. . . .
MIRACLE OR DESIGN?
LESSONS FROM THE
EAST ASIAN
EXPERIENCE

POLICY ESSAY NO.11

MIRACLE OR DESIGN?

LESSONS FROM THE EAST ASIAN EXPERIENCE

ALBERT FISHLOW
CATHERINE GWIN
STEPHAN HAGGARD
DANI RODRIK
ROBERT WADE

OVERSEAS DEVELOPMENT COUNCIL
WASHINGTON, DC

Library of Congress Cataloging-in-Publication Data

Wade, Robert.
    Miracle or design? lessons from the east asian experience/Robert Wade ... [et al.].

Policy Essay No. 11
Includes bibliographical references.
    1. East Asia—Economic conditions—Case studies. I. Wade, Robert. II. Series.

HC460.5.M56   1994   330.95—dc20   94-12155 CIP

ISBN: 1-56517-015-6

Printed in the United States of America.

Director of Publications: Christine E. Contee
Publications Editor: Jacqueline Edlund-Braun
Edited by Michael Treadway
Cover design: Snoreck Design Group
Book design: Tim Kenney Design Partners, Inc.

Contents

Foreword

When the World Bank, the largest and most influential development institution, evaluates the factors leading to the successful development of the world's most dynamic economies, the conclusions are bound to attract attention. The World Bank's recent study, *The East Asian Miracle: Economic Growth and Public Policy*, has rightly been subjected to considerable scrutiny around the world. The Bank's study not only analyzes the factors explaining East Asia's growth story, but also draws implications for other regions. At its root, the policy advocated is one of rapid export growth. But doubts can be raised about the basis for this conclusion as well as others. That is what this *Policy Essay* does.

Miracle or Design? Lessons from the East Asian Experience takes a critical look at what the World Bank's report says and what it does not say about the relevance of government intervention and other key policies in the East Asian "miracle" and about the miracle's applicability to others.

This eleventh volume in ODC's *Policy Essay* series is the latest in ODC's continuing body of work on the international institutions that affect development. Most recently, *Sustaining the Earth: Role of Multilateral Development Institutions* assessed the implications of the 1992 Earth Summit for the system of international development cooperation and set forth a roadmap of the five key multilateral institutions charged with following up on the summit. Later in 1994, a forthcoming *Policy Essay* will focus on strategies for multilateral development banks that support private sector development.

Miracle or Design? marks the first of a series of contributions to the *Policy Essay* series by ODC's newly created Program Advisory Group—in this instance, Stephan Haggard, Dani Rodrik, Robert Wade, and Albert Fishlow. Other members of this distinguished group include: Leszek Balcerowicz, Nancy Birdsall, Michael Bruno, Susan Collins, Rudi Dornbusch, Sebastian Edwards, Mohsin Khan, Robert Lawrence, Samuel Morley, Michael Mussa, Benno Ndulu, and Dwight Perkins.

The Overseas Development Council gratefully acknowledges The Ford Foundation and The Rockefeller Foundation for their support of the Council's overall program.

John W. Sewell
President
May 1994

Miracle or Design?
Lessons from the East Asian
Experience

Lessons from the
East Asian Experience

Albert Fishlow and Catherine Gwin

The countries of East Asia have achieved a remarkable record of sustained, rapid growth over the last thirty years. High rates of increase in income per capita began in Japan, spread to the "four tigers"—Hong Kong, Singapore, the Republic of Korea, and Taiwan—and have now become generalized across Indonesia, Malaysia, and Thailand. With an impressive expansion of its own in recent years, even mainland China has joined this group of what are now called the high-performing Asian economies (HPAEs).

Along with their rapid growth, these countries, which started thirty years ago with relatively equal land and income distributions, have succeeded in reducing inequality still further. As a result, human welfare and all the subordinate indices thereof (education, health, and housing, among others) have improved dramatically. This remarkable experience has occurred over a period long enough to rule out accident and with enough similarity of approach and outcome to rule out coincidence.

What is responsible for such a record, so starkly at variance with the performance of developing countries elsewhere? And what lessons are there for others to learn? These are the central questions posed in a recent World Bank study, *The East Asian Miracle: Economic Growth and Public Policy*.[1] The study is detailed, systematic, and informative. Most of what it describes has been known and written about by experts of the region for many years. Nonetheless, as a study undertaken by the world's leading development institution, it is a milestone product for at least three reasons.

First, the study brings together in one volume, certain to have a wide readership, a concise description of the equitable growth and development realized in East Asia during a period of time when such success was rarely achieved elsewhere.

Second, it pays closer attention to institutional arrangements as well as the dynamic interactions of economic factors than is typical of the Bank's previous assessments of development.

Third, the report represents an important acknowledgment by the World Bank that industrial policy, involving systematic government intervention in the market over extended periods of time, played a role in the rapid economic growth of the East Asian region. That experience clearly challenges the teachings of neoclassical economic theory and the prevailing policy wisdom advanced by the Bank itself and by its industrial-country member governments, except Japan.

Nonetheless, the report in the end is controversial—both in what it says and what it does not say about the relevance of government intervention in the East Asian "miracle" and about that miracle's applicability to others. The contributions in this *Policy Essay* address this controversy.

By way of background, this introduction briefly summarizes how the World Bank report came to be written and what it says about the East Asian experience; it then lays out two central disagreements over what the report concludes about the relevance of that experience for other developing countries. The three essays that follow, while recognizing the important advances made in the study, provide individually focused critiques of particular aspects of the report. They are intended not as a common response but as separate assessments. Indeed, the authors do not agree among themselves on all the points raised in the critiques.

THE IMPETUS OF THE REPORT

■ THE LAUNCH OF THE WORLD BANK STUDY was prompted most immediately by increasingly open criticism by the government of Japan of aspects of World Bank structural adjustment lending.[2] With this growing criticism came a determination on Japan's part to get the World Bank to pay greater attention to the distinctive features of the East Asian development experience, which stood in marked contrast to development approaches the Bank was then advocating in its loan conditionality and policy dialogues.

Japan began to express its disagreements with the World Bank openly in the late 1980s and early 1990s. For instance, a dispute between the two over Japan's support of subsidized loans to assist private-sector development in Southeast Asia highlighted a basic difference of approach: whereas the Japanese articulated the broad principle that financial policies should be subordinated to a wider industrial strategy, the Bank insisted on the principle that credit should be extended at market or nonsubsidized rates. Finding little support for its views within the Bank's management or among the other industrial-country members of its board, officials of the Japanese government broadened their critique of World Bank structural adjustment lending in a paper released in the fall of 1991.[3] The paper criticized what it viewed as an overemphasis on macroeconomic issues in Bank structural adjustment lending, and it argued, among other things, that 1) for a developing country to attain sustainable growth the government must adopt measures aimed directly at promoting investment; 2) the measures should be part of an explicit industrial policy designed to promote leading industries of the future; and 3) directed and subsidized credit has a key role to play in promoting industry because of extensive failures in developing-country markets.

Shortly after the release of this paper, Japan proposed that the Bank undertake a wide-ranging study of the East Asian development experience. The study would show, the Japanese held, that although successful development strategies require a healthy respect for market mechanisms, the role of government in industrial development should not be forgotten. At the 1991 World Bank annual meeting, Bank President Lewis

T. Preston announced the launch of the research project that became *The East Asian Miracle*; its total cost of more than $1.2 million would be largely financed by Japan, but the research itself would be led by World Bank staff with a limited number of outside experts.

. . . .

THE REPORT IN BRIEF

■   ACCORDING TO THE WORLD BANK REPORT, the causes of East Asia's remarkable growth are relatively straightforward. To cite the report: "In large measure, the HPAEs achieved high growth by getting the basics right" (p. 5).[4] This meant, first and foremost, the pursuit of macroeconomic stability, notably the control of inflation through prudent fiscal and monetary policies and stable and competitive exchange rates. Macroeconomic stability was considered important to promote confidence in the banking system and to encourage private firms to import advanced technologies from abroad. Getting the basics right also meant heavy and sustained public investment in social infrastructure, particularly education. A set of policies that the World Bank study labels "shared growth" entailed an emphasis on bringing education to all groups, not just the elites, and led to an accumulation of human capital, which in turn contributed to a high-quality civil service, an increasingly skilled labor force, and competent entrepreneurship.

A second key feature of East Asia's success, the report indicates, was early and continuing emphasis on the export of manufactures as a leading sector of growth. The "export push" ensured efficient allocation in the labor market of an increasingly skilled work force and made high rates of productivity growth possible. Exports permitted more-rapid acquisition of knowledge and access to best-practice technology. Also, exporting became the "standard by which all economic activity would be judged" (p. 324).

Third, the report acknowledges the special role of government intervention, particularly in the Northeast Asian pioneers: Japan, Taiwan, and Korea. The governments in these countries actively intervened to develop specific industries they saw as having high potential for growth and thus job creation. The policy instruments for this intervention included, among others, border measures (such as restrictions on imports and on foreign direct investment), preferential allocation of foreign exchange, tax incentives, subsidized loans, and exemption from antimonopoly laws. What was so unusual in these cases was not that intervention occurred but that it worked, unlike in the many similar efforts pursued by other developing countries over much the same period. Intervention, the report concedes, "resulted in higher and more equal growth than otherwise would have occurred" (p. 6). However, the report is quick to add that the impact on industrial development was limited and that "the prerequisites for success were so rigorous that policymakers seeking to follow similar paths in other developing economies have often met with failure" (p. 6).

Thus the report recognizes both the willingness and the ability of the Asian governments to intervene to positive effect. But it then rapidly seeks to downplay intervention's significance in East Asia and to reject intervention as a viable option for other countries. The reason given for that conclusion is that the special qualities required for successful intervention are not easily replicable. Two fundamental characteristics of the intervention process in East Asia are said to have been central. First, the costs of intervention were never allowed to become excessive. The interventions were both circumscribed and reversible. Financial controls were used, but not too much. Industrial protection was withdrawn when it became clear that an international market test of competitiveness could never be met, or when it had been. Second, institutional mechanisms somehow limited efforts to "pick winners" to cases where intervention had a positive return. When exports did not soon appear, there was little tendency to sustain governmental support. This is the key reason given in the report for why state intervention worked and the reason given for why it would not work elsewhere.

Moreover, the study argues that although intervention under these special circumstances could be effective, it was neither a powerful nor a necessary element of the East Asian miracle. The experience of Southeast Asia is cited to support this position. There the study finds far less intervention but, nevertheless, rapid growth.

In place of active intervention, the World Bank study emphasizes the importance of "market-friendly" development.[5] This approach recognizes the occasional need for an active state role—in instances where social return exceeds private gain and some degree of intervention can then make a large difference. It is different, therefore, from a laissez-faire strategy on the one hand and active industrial policy on the other. This middle ground leans toward the use of market forces wherever possible. And it sees the beauty of exports in the discipline of the competition which they entail.

Thus the World Bank report concludes that, along with the two other main features of the East Asian experience—macroeconomic stability and human resources investment—the "market oriented aspects of the East Asia's experience ... can be recommended with few reservations" (p. 26). But, the report goes on, "... the fact that interventions were an element of some of East Asia's economic success should not encourage selective intervention and should not become a reason to resist needed market-oriented reform" (p. 26).

Few development experts or policymakers are likely to quibble with the report's emphasis that getting the fundamentals right is a precondition of growth, or with its spotlighting of the process of "shared growth"—i.e., wide distribution of the gains from growth achieved through such measures as universal education, land reform, encouragement of small- and medium-size enterprises, etc. Indeed, this emphasis on "shared growth" appears to be more central than previous analysis has indicated. But there is reason to question the other conclusions that the World Bank report draws: about whether intervention can and should be used elsewhere, and about whether exports can provide so much of the answer for the still-emerging latecomers to industrial development.

. . . .

CAN SELECTIVE INTERVENTION WORK ELSEWHERE?

■   THE BANK'S CONTRIBUTION to explaining why intervention succeeded in East Asia comes down to its identification of a special contest mechanism that worked well in the cases of Japan, Korea, and Taiwan. What characterized this process were limits upon firm behavior jointly with restraints upon state participation:

[These countries] combined cooperative behavior—including sharing information among firms and between the private sectors, coordination of investment plans, and promotion of interdependent investments—with competition by firms to meet well defined economic performance criteria. They developed institutional structures in which firms competed for valued economic prizes ... in some dimensions while actively cooperating in others. (p. 93)

Such behavior required a state capable of defining an important role for itself in the development process. Not incidentally, it also required a state able to focus on important microeconomic decisions, free of constraints posed by large deficits, both budgetary and external. By insisting upon a reasonably balanced fiscal policy and by emphasizing exports rather than fixating on import substitution, the East Asian countries were able to escape important contradictions that afflicted many countries in Africa, South Asia, and Latin America. In particular, they avoided reliance on high rates of inflation and the resulting overvalued currencies and balance-of-payments difficulties.

There is little doubt that an important consequence of the limited growth that these other parts of the world have seen for well over a decade has been a recognition that macroeconomic stability is essential. And today, virtually everywhere, the transition to greater stability has either been accomplished or at the least is in process. Indeed, there is a tendency to overstate the earlier commitment to import substitution and the consequent macroeconomic disequilibrium in other countries. Many were already in the process of conversion away from reliance on the domestic market when the first oil shock occurred, and it was only the consequently expanded availability of foreign resources that reinforced reliance on the domestic market. The second shock in 1979 only aggravated the situation, and it has taken more than a decade for many countries to recover from the heavy borrowing that seemed a logical short-term strategy in 1974.

For these other countries, the massive intervention required to compensate for temporary macroeconomic disequilibria spilled over into a variety of microeconomic actions: direct subsidies, negative real interest rates, high tariffs, expansion of state enterprises, and selective availability of credit, among other measures. And these tended quickly to cancel each other out. As sector or industry A was given this or that privilege, so was sector or industry B, the result being to reduce the net gain to either and to simply weaken the state by contributing to larger and larger deficits.

Once there is both a commitment to macroeconomic equilibrium and larger and growing domestic savings, there is much greater scope for the state to sustain selective and productive intervention. Few would argue that (with the obvious exception of Hong Kong) the East Asian economies have failed to provide such stimuli for selected sectors. The evidence against the capacity of other countries to do so is derived from an earlier period during which macroeconomic policy was badly managed. That is not a fair test. If, in fact, countries are now competent to maintain macroeconomic policies long sought and long advocated, why not assume that the same competence extends to industrial policy? A small state can be a more powerful state, and selecting particular areas for promotion can pay off. That, after all, is one of the few advantages of backwardness: one can perceive what other, more advanced countries have done and seek to replicate it. From this perspective, it is clear that there are important aspects of the HPAEs' experience that warrant rather more analysis than provided by the World Bank study.

. . . .
CAN EXPORTS LEAD THE WAY?

■ ANOTHER OF THE REPORT'S MAIN MESSAGES, given its con-clusion that intervention is likely to prove unproductive where there have been past errors, is that a key replicable part of East Asia's success is reliance on rapid export growth:

> Finally, we found that a successful export push, whether it results from an open economy and strong economic fundamentals, or from a combination of strong fundamentals and prudently-chosen interventions, offers high eco-nomic gains. Of all the interventions we surveyed, those to promote exports were the most readily compatible with a wide diversity of economic circum-stances. (p. 367)

In order to reach this conclusion, two subordinate questions had to be answered implicitly in the affirmative. First, is the world market big enough to absorb the implied increase in exports of manufactured products? Second, is it open enough? That is, can developing countries use export-push strategies in a world ever more prone to defensive reaction on the part of the industrial countries?

On the first question, the major argument reduces to the small size of developing-country exports of manufactures relative to the intended markets. Despite the East Asian countries' success, total 1988 imports of their manufactures by the European Community, the United States, and Japan amounted in 1988 to only 3.1 percent of the total of those three markets; even if *all* the developing countries in the world had expanded their exports at the same rate as the East Asian countries, their share of that total would have amounted to only 3.7 percent (p. 361). Hence, there appears to be ample room for continuing expansion. And one should not forget the corresponding expansion in imports that more-rapid growth makes possible—export-led expansion need not be unbalanced.

On the second question, the Bank recognizes that developing countries are under pressure in world markets to conform to industrial-country standards. Some of the policies that the East Asian economies pursued successfully in decades past would no longer be tolerated by the industrial countries today. Let us remember that the United States underwrote the export expansion first of Japan, and later of the rest of the East Asian group, as part of a broader security strategy involving the entire region. One need only look at the efforts in the Uruguay Round to limit developing-country latitude in the areas of intellectual property, for example, to note the difference between the 1960s and the 1990s. Those who come later will clearly encounter more difficulty in pushing exports than did the pioneers. Although the export market remains an important option, it cannot be the sole route.

The report thus exaggerates what is realistically possible when it imagines all follower countries pursuing an export-led strategy. There is an important difference between eliminating handicaps to the expansion of exports and acting aggressively to push them as the mainstay of future progress. Indeed, in the case of Japan the export-push strategy was motivated by the need to increase foreign-exchange earnings, but trade has constituted only a relatively small share of Japan's GNP; the expansion of domestic markets was far more important for growth—a point that the study fails to analyze adequately.

Country size makes a difference in defining a correct approach. What may be much more appropriate for larger developing countries is an *export-adequate* development path, plus openness to foreign direct investment (which has made a major contribution to growth in Southeast Asia). This strategy recognizes the difficulty in today's competitive trade policy environment, of replicating growth of exports on the order of 10 to 15 percent per year, and of expanding the export sector to as large a percentage of GDP as the East Asian countries have been able to. A regular annual growth of exports on the order of 1 or 2 percentage points above GDP expansion ensures important advantages: the advancement of productivity in the exporting industries, and therefore in others as well, needed to compete with other suppliers; the establishment of an important objective measure of relative success in manufacturing technology; the maintenance of a competitive exchange rate, which avoids overvaluation and eventual macroeconomic difficulties; the avoidance of *excessive* foreign borrowing, with its negative effects on domestic savings capacity as well as on exchange rates; and finally, the evolution of institutional rules capable of ensuring continuing success.

There may well still be smaller economies fully capable of matching the impressive East Asian accomplishments in the export sector. But for others, especially those with primary-products exports of central importance in their total sales and with limited saving capacity, East Asia's success holds out an improbable lesson.

. . . .

THE THREE ESSAYS

■   THE THREE ESSAYS THAT FOLLOW are different attempts to evaluate the Bank's report. Their tone is critical; but implicitly, and sometimes explicitly, all three acknowledge positive contributions of the study. Where they all differ from the Bank's position, however, is in their reading of the report as overemphasizing the market system as the key to East Asian success. Each author then provides his own reading of that undeniable success.

Dani Rodrik stresses that the central and strong conclusions relating to the positive role of exports and the negative contribution of industrial policy are not proven by the Bank's report. He argues, first, that initial conditions, particularly the relatively high degree of equality found in the Asian economies, were extraordinarily favorable to development; that of course leaves one with the problem of what to do with the many other developing countries that lack that advantage. Second, Rodrik evaluates the report's analysis of industrial policy, paying special attention to the methodology the report employs. He finds serious difficulty with the report's attempts to negate the possible importance of industrial policy. Third, he finds the report's emphasis on exports excessive, and in particular he exposes an underlying weakness in the statistical analysis used to establish a positive association between economic openness and growth. More broadly, he criticizes the report for claiming much and establishing precious little in this critical area. Finally, Rodrik questions the report's apparent acceptance of the styles of governance in the East Asian economies, citing in part the substantial evidence of high-placed corruption that has characterized them.

Robert Wade takes a more focused look at the study and concludes that it does not establish convincingly that selective industrial policies were unimportant for the economic success of Northeast Asia. The report adduces four main types of evidence for this proposition, none of which survives serious scrutiny, Wade argues. His lesson for other countries is that while market forces should be relied on to play the main allocative role, there are good reasons, based on both historical experience and recent theoretical work, why these market forces should be governed by a long-term, supply-side national industrial strategy—just as major corporations routinely plan their own future within the market system. Other developing countries should pay careful attention to how the Northeast Asian countries managed to conduct such strategies successfully.

Stephan Haggard, a political scientist, focuses on the Bank's analysis of government institutions and politics. Overall, he endorses as "refreshingly frank" the report's discussion of labor policy, business-government relations, and the importance of bureaucratic insulation from special interests. However, he also finds serious limitations in the report's political analysis and an unwillingness to draw firmer conclusions about institutional design. Among the central problems is the relationship between authoritarianism and rapid growth in East Asia; the report spends little time on this uncomfortable fact. Second, although a call for economic reform is at the core of the report, Haggard finds surprisingly little discussion of how reforms were initiated and sustained in these economies. He endorses the idea that "shared growth" was important, but he argues that reform was possible because of major institutional changes, particularly the concentration of executive and bureaucratic power. In short, strong states were central to East Asia's market-friendly approach. Haggard concludes by considering the international political context of today, including the pressure on developing countries to open markets and conform to developed–country economic and political standards, and wonders about the freedom of other developing countries to follow even its recommendation of rapid export growth.

Clearly, the World Bank study is a useful beginning toward understanding the lessons that can be learned from East Asia and applied in other developing countries very much in search of their own miracles. But it is not the final word.

N o t e s

[1] World Bank, *The East Asian Miracle: Economic Growth and Public Policy* (New York: Oxford University Press for the World Bank, 1993).

[2] See Robert Wade, "The World Bank and the Art of Paradigm Maintenance: *The East Asian Miracle* as a Response to Japan's Attempts to Recalibrate the Rules of the International Economy," unpublished paper, Institute of Development Studies, Sussex University, 1994.

[3] Overseas Economic Cooperation Fund, "Issues Related to the World Bank's Approach to Structural Adjustment: A Proposal From a Major Partner," *OECF Occasional Papers* No. 1, October 1991.

[4] Throughout this volume, page numbers cited without further reference in the text are those of *The East Asian Miracle* (World Bank, op. cit.).

[5] This view is also found in World Bank, *World Development Report 1991: The Challenge of Development* (New York: Oxford University Press for the World Bank, 1991).

Chapter 1

King Kong Meets Godzilla: The World Bank and *The East Asian Miracle*

Dani Rodrik

There exists probably no greater challenge in the area of economic development than that of explaining how eight East Asian economies (Japan, the Republic of Korea, Taiwan, Singapore, Hong Kong, Indonesia, Malaysia, and Thailand) managed to increase their per capita incomes at an annual average rate of 5.5 percent during 1965–1990, considerably faster than any other developing region. Despite a large body of research, there is little consensus on the role that public policies have played in this performance. Some have seen in the East Asian experience the vindication of market-oriented ideas, whereas others have emphasized the role of government intervention in the trade and industrial arenas. Even the facts—how much intervention has there really been?—have been in dispute.

As the world's leading multilateral lending institution, the World Bank has advocated, at least since the late 1970s, a minimalist role for government. This stance leaves the Bank vulnerable to criticism from those who point to the East Asian model as a case of successful state activism. Now, however, the Bank has confronted the East Asian experience head on, with its 400-page report *The East Asian Miracle: Economic Growth and Public Policy,* released in 1993. The confrontation, like the clash of celluloid titans—the King Kong of 1818 H Street versus the Godzilla of the Ginza—makes for a fascinating spectacle. The Bank emerges bloodied, but as the self-declared victor of the encounter.

The East Asian Miracle makes it official that most of the high-performing Asian economies (HPAEs, as the report calls them) have had extensive government intervention. It also grants that some of these interventions, in the areas of credit and exports, may have worked to foster both growth and equity. These concessions alone make the publication of the report a watershed event. Although these conclusions will certainly not come as a surprise to most close observers of the East Asian economies, to date much of the policy-oriented economics community has steadfastly questioned their validity. Thanks to the Bank's study, it will no longer be fashionable to argue that the East Asian economies did so well because their governments intervened so little, or that they would have grown even faster had their governments intervened less. This is an extremely valuable service, because the debate on East Asia can now move on to a higher plateau of common understanding.

What the report itself does with these basic findings is more controversial. Even as it acknowledges extensive government activism, the Bank finds in the East Asian experience a confirmation of its "market-friendly" approach to policy, encompassing macroeconomic stability, human capital formation, openness to international trade, and an environment that fosters private investment and competition. It also argues that most of the interventions that worked in the HPAEs are either too risky or too impractical in the 1990s for other developing countries to imitate. (So-called export-push strategies are exempted from this blanket recommendation against intervention.) In sum, the Bank finds no lessons for itself from the HPAEs' experience that it had not already learned.

The World Bank has a well-deserved reputation for putting out readable yet analytical studies, rich in statistical information and institutional detail. *The East Asian Miracle* is no exception. These features help convey the Bank's work and its policy conclusions to a broad audience. The report has already been widely covered in the press, and its conclusions have been cited in scholarly works. At the same time, however, this visibility places a heavy burden on the Bank. Conclusions must be well supported, and when definitive answers cannot be provided, this should be acknowledged. In this respect, *The East Asian Miracle* does not measure up as well. Upon closer look, some of the critical bits of analysis contained in the report turn out to be weak and questionable. Consequently, many of its conclusions and recommendations, those relating to trade and industrial strategy in particular, have to be discounted heavily.

In a review that is necessarily short in relation to the report itself, it is impossible to cover all aspects of the study. Nor is there any need to, because there is much in the report that is sensible and unobjectionable. This essay will therefore focus mostly on disagreements, differences in emphases, and quarrels about method.

The essay begins, in the section that follows, by emphasizing the importance of initial conditions, concerning income and wealth equality and educational levels, to the HPAEs' takeoff. In particular, I argue that the report does not sufficiently emphasize the importance of the initial equality in the distribution of resources that was typical of the HPAEs. Once this initial equality is taken into account, in a statistical sense there is nothing miraculous about the HPAEs' growth performance. Next I evaluate the report's arguments on industrial policy, after which the discussion turns to the report's preoccupation with exports. Here the focus is on evaluating the report's conceptual framework and analysis. I argue that there are serious shortcomings in the way that the report has approached industrial policies and export promotion strategies. The focus then turns to governance issues: I discuss some puzzles raised by the HPAEs' experience, related in particular to their special styles of governance and the prevalence of corruption. The final section of the essay offers some concluding comments.

. . . .

INITIAL CONDITIONS: THE IMPORTANCE OF EQUALITY AND EDUCATION

■   IN SEARCHING FOR THE SECRETS of the East Asian miracle, the obvious first place to look is the set of initial conditions that preceded economic takeoff. There are two respects, not entirely unrelated, in which the HPAEs differed substantially by 1960 from other developing countries at similar levels of development. First, the HPAEs were considerably better positioned with regard to schooling and educational attainment (and, by implication, had a significantly more skilled labor force). Second, the degree of economic inequality, as measured by the distribution of income or of land ownership, was uncommonly low. Because the HPAEs clearly stood out in these respects before their performance started to diverge from that of other developing countries, a reasonable hypothesis is that these initial conditions are causally linked to their subsequent stellar performance.

Table 1 gives an idea of the extent to which the HPAEs were already outliers by the early 1960s with respect to human capital and associated demographic indicators. The table presents the differences between actual values of these indicators and the values predicted by a cross-country statistical analysis that relates these indicators to per capita income. We find, for example, that whereas all of the HPAEs except Indonesia had virtually universal primary schooling by 1960, the cross-country benchmark puts the expected primary enrollment levels 30 to 40 percentage points lower in the cases of Korea, Malaysia, Singapore, and Taiwan. Similarly, secondary enrollment rates were considerably higher in Japan, Korea, and Taiwan than in countries in other parts of the world at similar levels of income. All but Singapore stood out in having exceptionally high literacy rates. (Note, however, that the educational indicators used here measure flows, or additions to human capital, rather than the stock of human capital itself.) Finally, fertility and mortality rates were almost uniformly lower than in countries with similar incomes, indicating an earlier demographic transition. There can be little doubt that the HPAEs were in a class of their own by 1960 in terms of educational and demographic indicators.

The same is true with respect to wealth and income distribution. Table 2 lists the available Gini coefficients for income and land distribution for the HPAEs and a sample of comparator countries. (The Gini coefficient, a statistical measure of income or wealth distribution, is widely used in economic analysis.) The coefficients are selected from surveys undertaken as close to 1960 as possible, so that they portray once again the initial

Economy	Primary Enrollment Ratio (1960)			Secondary Enrollment Ratio (1960)			Literacy Rate (1960)			Fertility Rate (1965)			Mortality Rate (1965)		
	Actual	Pre-dicted	Differ-ence	Actual	Pre-dicted	Differ-ence	Actual	Pre-dicted	Differ-ence	Actual	Pre-dicted	Differ-ence	Actual	Pre-dicted	Differ-ence
Hong Kong	0.87	0.83	0.04	0.24	0.23	0.01	0.70	0.59	0.11	4.50	5.23	-0.73	0.03	0.08	-0.06
Indonesia	0.67	0.51	0.16	0.06	0.07	-0.01	0.39	0.25	0.15	5.50	6.48	-0.98	0.14	0.14	-0.00
Japan	1.03	0.92	0.11	0.74	0.29	0.45	0.98	0.70	0.28	2.00	4.80	-2.80	0.02	0.07	-0.05
Korea	0.94	0.57	0.37	0.27	0.10	0.17	0.71	0.31	0.40	4.80	6.27	-1.47	0.06	0.13	-0.07
Malaysia	0.96	0.68	0.28	0.19	0.15	0.04	0.53	0.43	0.10	6.30	5.84	0.46	0.06	0.11	-0.06
Singapore	1.11	0.78	0.33	0.32	0.21	0.11	0.50	0.54	-0.04	4.70	5.42	-0.72	0.03	0.09	-0.07
Taiwan	0.96	0.62	0.34	0.28	0.12	0.15	0.54	0.36	0.18	4.80	6.08	-1.28	0.02	0.12	-0.10
Thailand	0.83	0.57	0.26	0.12	0.10	0.02	0.68	0.31	0.37	6.30	6.27	0.03	0.09	0.13	-0.04

Note: Predicted values of the indicators were obtained from a cross-country regression run on a 118-country sample, with per capita GDP in 1960 and its square used as independent variables.

Sources: Author's calculations based on original data from Alan Heston and Robert Summers, "A New Set of International Comparisons of Real Product and Price Levels: Estimates for 134 Countries," Review of Income and Wealth, Vol. 34, 1988, pp. 1–25; Robert Barro and Holger Wolf, "Data Appendix for Economic Growth in a Cross-Section of Countries," unpublished paper, Harvard University, 1989.

TABLE 2. DISTRIBUTIONAL INDICATORS FOR HPAEs AND SELECTED COMPARATOR COUNTRIES, AROUND 1960

Economy	Gini Coefficient for Income	Gini Coefficient for Land
HPAEs		
Hong Kong	0.49	n.a.
Indonesia	0.33	n.a.
Japan	0.40	0.47
Korea	0.34	0.39
Malaysia	0.42	0.47
Singapore	0.40	n.a.
Taiwan	0.31	0.46
Thailand	0.41	0.46
Unweighted average	0.39	0.45
COMPARATORS		
Argentina	0.44	0.87
Brazil	0.53	0.85
Egypt	0.42	0.67
India	0.42	0.52
Kenya	0.64	0.69
Mexico	0.53	0.69
Philippines	0.45	0.53
Turkey	0.56	0.59
Unweighted average	0.50	0.68

Note: n.a., not available.

Sources: Original data are from Shail Jain, Size Distribution of Income: A Compilation of Data *(Washington, DC: World Bank, 1975); Gary Fields, "A Compendium of Data on Inequality and Poverty for the Developing World," unpublished manuscript, Cornell University, 1989; C.L. Taylor and M.C. Hudson,* World Handbook of Political and Social Indicators, *2nd ed. (New Haven, CT: Yale University Press, 1972). For dates and further details of the calculations, Alberto Alesina and Dani Rodrick, "Distributive Politics and Economic Growth,"* Quarterly Journal of Economics *(forthcoming).*

conditions prior to economic takeoff. We see a striking degree of equality in the HPAEs compared with other developing countries. The HPAE with the highest degree of income inequality (Hong Kong) still lies below the average for the non–East Asian comparator countries. The differences are even greater for land distribution: Japan and Malaysia, with the greatest inequality in land distribution among the HPAEs for which data are available, still exhibited a more equal distribution than any of the comparators listed. These findings reflect, in large part, the land reforms undertaken in Japan, Korea, and Taiwan prior to 1960. But Indonesia, Malaysia, Thailand, and Singapore (a city-state) also had comparatively egalitarian distributions.

To gauge the importance of these initial conditions to subsequent growth, Table 3 presents the results of some cross-country growth regressions similar in spirit to those in Table 1.8 of the World Bank report. The basic growth regression in the report includes gross domestic product (GDP) per capita in 1960 (relative to the United States), primary and secondary enrollment rates in 1960, the average investment-GDP ratio over 1960–1985, and population growth rate over 1960–1985 as the explanatory variables. Average per capita GDP growth over 1960–1985 is the dependent variable. The first column of Table 3 reproduces this basic regression for the smaller sample of 41 countries for which both Gini coefficients are available.[1] The basic findings are the same, save for a larger adjusted R^2 in the smaller sample: initial income and the investment rate are statistically the strongest determinants of cross-country growth performance. The regression reported in the second column drops the secondary enrollment ratio and population growth variables, which are both statistically insignificant (here as well as in the report) and adds the Gini coefficients for income and land distribution (measured around 1960). Both of the Gini coefficients enter with a statistically significant negative sign, and the fit of the regression improves considerably (the adjusted R^2 increases from 0.46 to 0.67). Hence the initial level of equality is an important determinant of subsequent growth.

The trouble with a regression like the last one, however, is that the average investment rate during 1960–1985 can hardly be considered an exogenous determinant of growth. For one thing, growth itself may be partly responsible for the high investment rate. For another, even if investment is truly exogenous with respect to growth, explaining growth by appealing to physical capital accumulation is not entirely satisfactory. An adequate accounting for growth requires developing an understanding of the accumulation as well. In fact, Alwyn Young has argued that the East Asian newly industrializing economies stand out mostly in their investment rates (and in the increase in their labor force participation

	Dependent Variables			
Independent Variable	Per Capita Growth (1960–1985)			
	(1)	(2)	(3)	(4)
Intercept	1.07	4.21*	6.22*	3.71*
	(0.64)	(3.50)	(4.69)	(3.86)
Per Capita GDP (1960)	−0.61*	−0.50*	−0.38*	−0.38*
	(−3.83)	(−4.92)	(−3.25)	(−3.61)
Primary Enrollment (1960)	0.84	1.28	2.66**	3.85*
	(0.70)	(1.43)	(2.66)	(4.88)
Secondary Enrollment (1960)	0.83			
	(0.46)			
Investment-GDP Ratio (1960–1985)	13.06*	12.50*		
	(3.44)	(4.13)		
Population Growth (1960–1985)	−38.37			
	(−1.10)			
Gini Coefficient for Land		−2.60**	−5.22*	−5.50*
		(−2.20)	(−4.38)	(−5.24)
Gini Coefficient for Income		−5.28*	3.47	
		(−3.22)	(−1.82)	
Adjusted R^2	0.46	0.67	0.53	0.53

(continued next page)

rates), and that their productivity growth rates are not extraordinary.[2] This places an even greater premium on being able to explain the HPAEs' high investment rates.

For these reasons, the remaining regressions treat investment as an endogenous variable. The regression reported in the third column of Table 3 drops investment as a regressor and focuses only on the role of exogenous initial conditions—namely, per capita income, primary enrollment, and income and land distribution, all measured in or around 1960. This regression does quite well, with an adjusted R^2 of 0.53. Even though the significance of the coefficient on income distribution is reduced

TABLE 3. CONTINUED

Independent Variable	Dependent Variables	
	Investment-Ratio GDP (1960–1985)	Population Growth (1960–1985)
	(5)	(6)
Intercept	16.06**	2.41*
	(2.64)	(3.24)
Per Capita GDP (1960)	0.94	−0.22*
	(1.76)	(−3.44)
Primary Enrollment (1960)	11.01**	−1.68*
	(2.40)	(−3.00)
Secondary Enrollment (1960)		
Investment-GDP Ratio (1960–1985)		
Population Growth (1960–1985)		
Gini Coefficient for Land	−21.04*	1.50**
	(−3.85)	(2.24)
Gini Coefficient for Income	14.44	1.38
	(1.66)	(1.30)
Adjusted R^2	0.43	0.63

Notes: The sample is restricted to countries for which distributional indicators are available. The number of observations was 41 in all regressions except (4), where it was 49. The numbers in parentheses are t-statistics. Asterisks denote levels of statistical significance; * = significant at the 1 percent confidence level; ** = significant at the 5 percent confidence level.

Sources: See Tables 1 and 2 in this chapter.

to the 10 percent level, the coefficient on land distribution becomes even more significant, and the primary enrollment ratio is now significant for the first time. The coefficient on the Gini coefficient for land indicates that an increase in this indicator from, say, 0.4 to 0.5 would reduce subsequent growth by 0.5 percentage point per year. It is striking that such a parsimonious characterization of the initial conditions—in terms of income, education, and equity levels alone—can explain more than 50 percent of the variation in subsequent growth rates in the sample.[3]

The next two columns of Table 3 show that these initial conditions also play an important role in determining investment rates and population growth. The primary enrollment rate and the Gini coefficient for land enter significantly in both regressions. High levels of education and low inequality at the outset are associated with a high investment share of GDP and low population growth. These results underscore the point made above regarding the endogeneity of investment, and the inappropriateness of using it (as well as population growth) as a separate regressor.

How much of the actual growth of the HPAEs can the initial levels of school enrollment and equality explain? This question is answered in Table 4 for five of the eight HPAEs (those for which land Gini coefficients are available). The answer is, quite a lot of it. Around 90 percent or more of the growth of Korea, Taiwan, Malaysia, and Thailand can be accounted for by these economies' exceptionally high levels of primary school enrollment and equality around 1960. The corresponding proportion for Japan is only about three-quarters—largely because Japan's investment rate is underpredicted by the initial conditions. (Once investment is controlled for, Japan's predicted growth rate matches the actual very closely.) But none of the HPAEs is too far off from the regression line. In fact, by adding initial equality, our simple regression tracks the HPAEs' performance much better than the report's basic growth regression (which does particularly poorly in explaining growth in Korea, Taiwan, and Thailand; see Table 4)—this even though the latter contains additional variables like investment and population growth. Thus, once initial levels of schooling and equality are taken into account, there appears to be nothing miraculous about the HPAEs' growth experience.

This point is driven home by looking at the differences in actual and predicted growth for the comparator countries listed in Table 4. These differences tend to be much larger for these countries. For example, the predicted growth rates for Argentina, India, and the Philippines are two to three times higher than the actual rates. Brazil's growth, on the other hand, is greatly underestimated. These results are interesting because they suggest that the "growth puzzles" are not the HPAEs but rather countries like Argentina, the Philippines, and Brazil, which are the true outliers once initial conditions are controlled for.

Why did the initial conditions matter so much? The importance of human capital for growth is well recognized and does not need much discussion. Human capital makes investment more productive, facilitates the transfer and adoption of advanced technology from abroad, and enables the establishment of a meritocratic, efficient, and capable public administration.

The links between initial equality and growth are less certain and have only recently been examined in some detail. Initial results by Persson and Tabellini and by Alesina and Rodrik on the negative relationship between inequality and growth have been shown to be statistically robust by Clarke.[4] There are several arguments regarding the specific causal linkages. Murphy, Shleifer, and Vishny have argued that a sufficiently equal distribution of income is a prerequisite for industrialization, because the middle class is the natural source of demand for home-based manufactures.[5] Their analysis is in fact motivated by the experience of economies such as Japan and Taiwan, where demand by farmers for manufactures apparently played an important role during the early stages of industrialization.[6]

Other arguments are primarily political in nature. Alesina and Rodrik have pointed out that, as long as the preferences of the majority carry political weight, there will be more pressure to redistribute income and wealth in societies where inequities are large.[7] Such pressures will ordinarily result in various kinds of redistributive policies that are harmful to private investment and to growth. Alesina and Perotti argue that the link may also operate through political instability: inequality results in demands to alter the established order; political instability in turn reduces investment. They also provide empirical evidence consistent with this view.[8]

Whatever the relative merits of these theoretical arguments, it seems quite plausible that the relative equality of income and wealth in the HPAEs has been a critical determinant of the quality of policymaking there. It is doubtful whether the single-minded pursuit of economic growth that has been a characteristic of many of the HPAEs (particularly Japan, Korea, Taiwan, and Singapore) could have been maintained in an environment where distributional issues were salient.[9] The inequality of income in Latin America has often been mentioned as a source of the region's macroeconomic instability and periodic populist cycles. Significant income inequality:

TABLE 4. PER CAPITA ANNUAL GROWTH RATES FOR HPAEs AND SELECTED COMPARATOR COUNTRIES, ACTUAL AND PREDICTED, FOR 1960-1985

Economy	Actual Growth	Regression (2) from Table 3 (Investment Included as Regressor)		Regression (3) from Table 3 (Investment Not Included as Regressor)		Proportion Explained in World Bank Report (percent)
		Predicted Growth	Proportion Explained (percent)	Predicted Growth	Proportion Explained (percent)	
HPAEs						
Japan	5.76	5.59	97	4.26	74	82
Korea	5.95	5.06	85	5.24	88	63
Malaysia	4.52	4.36	96	4.44	98	87
Taiwan	5.68	4.77	84	4.96	87	58
Thailand	4.06	3.83	94	4.34	107	66

(continued next page)

TABLE 4. CONTINUED

Economy	Actual Growth	Regression (2) from Table 3 (Investment Included as Regressor)		Regression (3) from Table 3 (Investment Not Included as Regressor)		Proportion Explained in World Bank Report (percent)
		Predicted Growth	Proportion Explained (percent)	Predicted Growth	Proportion Explained (percent)	
COMPARATORS						
Argentina	0.48	2.52	525	1.58	329	n.a.
Brazil	3.52	2.63	75	1.96	56	n.a.
Egypt	3.49	2.90	83	2.83	81	n.a.
India	1.37	3.26	238	3.46	253	n.a.
Kenya	0.96	1.59	166	1.46	152	n.a.
Mexico	2.46	2.03	83	2.08	85	n.a.
Philippines	1.77	3.11	176	4.08	231	n.a.
Turkey	2.81	2.59	92	2.71	96	n.a.

Notes: n.a., not available. Predicted growth rates are calculated by applying the coefficient estimates reported in columns (2) and (3) of Table 3 to each country's actual data for initial income level, enrollment ratio, distributional indicators, and investment levels.

Sources: Author's calculations; Robert Barro and Holger Wolf, "Data Appendix for Economic Growth in a Cross-Section of Countries," unpublished paper, Harvard University, 1989.

leads to social pressures that governments have attempted to relieve through populist policies. After one or two years of economic expansion inflation soars, real wages fall, unemployment starts to increase, and output declines. The policies prove unsustainable, and the government has to switch to another set of policies. Many countries in the [Latin American] region have suffered this populist cycle, some of them more than once. In East Asia, the situation has been the opposite. A very equitable income distribution has facilitated macroeconomic stability.[10]

In his comparison of the responses of East Asian and Latin American countries to the debt crisis, Sachs has similarly focused on income equality as a determinant of the quality of macroeconomic management.[11]

This is an area where clearly more work is required. But there are good reasons to believe that many of the microeconomic and macroeconomic policies common to the HPAEs, and cited in the World Bank report as components of the so-called market-friendly approach (such as macroeconomic stability and reasonably minor microeconomic distortions), have been greatly facilitated by the relative equality of income and wealth.

In view of the apparent centrality of distributional preconditions, the report's treatment of the issue is quite skimpy.[12] There is a short description of land reform and its favorable implications for growth (pp. 160–61), but the arguments are superficial and in the nature of afterthoughts.[13] This is not to say that the report ignores distribution. To the contrary, there is a great deal of emphasis on how equity and growth went hand-in-hand—the "shared growth" phenomenon. What the report lacks is a serious discussion of equity as a precondition of growth. Among all the explanations offered in the report for the success of the HPAEs, a relatively equal initial distribution of income and wealth hardly figures.[14]

The report also downplays the role of the HPAEs' initial advantage in education. It argues that most of the difference between HPAEs and other countries in human capital formation is accounted for by changes that took place after 1960, and not by the difference in initial conditions (pp. 198–99). This is a deceptive argument that ignores the fact that high-growth countries will naturally experience higher rates of physical and human capital formation. If the initial advantage placed the HPAEs on a higher growth path, there is little surprise in learning that the gap widened considerably over time.

DID ACTIVIST TRADE AND INDUSTRIAL
POLICIES MATTER?

■   NO ASPECT OF THE EAST ASIAN EXPERIENCE is more controversial than the role played by interventionist industrial policies. Controversy surrounds both the extent of intervention that actually took place and its effectiveness. As noted at the beginning of this essay, *The East Asian Miracle* represents a bold step for the World Bank, certainly in relation to its previous stance: the report acknowledges that intervention was extensive in practically all of the HPAEs (save for Hong Kong), and that it was at best quite successful and at worst rather harmless. In my judgment, this represents a sensible starting point for a new conventional wisdom about the East Asian experience. It seems far closer to the truth than previous arguments that portrayed these countries either as paragons of market liberalism or as instances of government-driven industrialization.

The report's more detailed conclusions on what worked and what did not are more problematic. The reason is that the analytical framework employed in analyzing the consequences of industrial policies is riddled with crater-sized holes.

The problems begin with the authors' classification of interventionist policies into the following three categories: "promotion of specific industries," "mild financial repression combined with directed credit," and "export push" (see pp. 24–25 and Chapter 6 of the report). The first of these is judged to have been ineffective (and hence not worth emulating in other countries), the second to have been successful in certain instances (but too risky or impractical to implement in other contexts), and the third to have been the most successful of all (and hence the most promising for other countries as well).

This categorization is curious because it makes no distinction between policy *instruments* and policy *goals*. "Promotion of specific industries" is a policy goal, in pursuit of which a government can deploy various instruments. Two such instruments are directed credit and export subsidies, the other two items on the list! Indeed, the country summaries on industrial policy (pp. 306–312 of the report) amply demonstrate that credit and export policies were among the foremost instruments used to implement sectoral priorities. To say that directed credit and export-push policies worked, whereas promotion of specific industries did not, is a logical inconsistency of major proportions. It is difficult to fathom how it found its way into the report (and as a major conclusion, to boot). Where was credit directed, if not to specific industries?[15] Whose exports were pushed, if not those of exportable-goods industries? And how is it possible to judge selective industrial policies a failure if at the same time directed credit and export-push policies were successful?[16]

The analysis that backs up the conclusion about the inefficacy of industrial promotion policies—the first of the three conclusions mentioned above—is equally curious. First, as the reader may have guessed already from the above discussion, the analysis does not actually try to ascertain the effectiveness of any of the specific policy instruments used to promote targeted industries. (This is done indirectly—and casually—in the discussion on credit market and export policies, which, as mentioned above, are treated as distinct areas.) Instead, the authors pose two questions, which they proceed to answer in the negative: Did high-wage or high-value-added industries expand faster than would have been predicted on the basis of cross-country evidence or factor endowments? And was productivity growth more rapid in the promoted sectors than in others? A closer look at these questions is warranted, because there are serious shortcomings in both their operationalization and the interpretation attached to the results.

DID INDUSTRIAL POLICY INFLUENCE STRUCTURAL CHANGE?

The report compares the changes in industrial structure observed in the HPAEs with Hollis Chenery–like norms obtained from cross-country regressions. The conclusion is that two sectors stand out in the HPAEs as regards relative size and growth: metal products and electronics and machinery; and textiles and garments. The continued preponderance of textiles and garments in the HPAEs' output is then adduced as evidence that governments' efforts to move into more capital-intensive industries must have been largely ineffective:

In Korea, for example, despite the government's extensive efforts to speed the private sector's shift from labor-intensive to capital- and technology-intensive industries, the relatively labor-intensive textiles and garments sector was nearly three times bigger than international norms predicted in 1988, a substantial increase relative to international norms from 1968. During the same period, Korea merely maintained the international norm in chemicals, a heavily promoted sector; while other heavily promoted sectors, basic metals and metal products and machinery, achieved only modest improvements. (pp. 312–13)

One can quarrel with many aspects of this conclusion. Because the report does not systematically analyze specific policies and their consequences, it is difficult to read much into broad sectoral changes. Amsden, for example, points out that the textile industry was heavily promoted in Japan in at least part of the relevant period.[17] The textile industry was also one of the industries designated as strategic in Korea during the 1960s.[18] Further, the report examines only broad groupings of industries as represented by standard two-digit classification codes; this level of aggregation may be too coarse to discern much of the intended structural change (for more on this subject see Robert Wade's essay in this volume). Many subsectors within the broader textiles industry are certainly capital- and technology-intensive.

Perhaps the most serious objection is that cross-country norms about sectoral configurations necessarily carry little weight in economies where reliance on foreign trade has been significantly greater than elsewhere. As the share of foreign trade in the HPAEs' incomes rose, it is only natural that the forces of specialization exerted by comparative advantage would have become stronger. Given the very different trade strategy followed by other developing countries, their experience does not provide an adequate counterfactual. An analysis such as that in the report cannot tell us anything about what the effects of industrial policies have been, because we do not know what the outcome would have been in their absence. To put it more concretely, had government policies been truly ineffective, it is entirely possible that the share of textiles and clothing would have become even larger.

The report next looks at the pattern of correlations between growth in sectoral shares of value added and sectoral wages or value added per worker. The motivation for doing so, as far as I can make it out, seems to be the following sequence of arguments: 1) changes in industrial structure can come about because of either market-driven reasons (which are associated with comparative advantage and factor endowments) or selective government promotion policies; 2) HPAEs' comparative advantage resides in labor-intensive sectors; 3) selective government policy in HPAEs has favored capital- and technology-intensive industries; 4) sectoral levels of wages and value added per worker are indicators of sectoral capital and technology intensities; 5) therefore, if factor endowments (i.e., markets) predominated as a causal force in structural change, growth in sectoral shares of value added should have been negatively correlated with sectoral wages and value added per worker, whereas the opposite should have been the case if government policies predominated.

The findings are as follows. The results for Japan, Hong Kong, and Taiwan do not reveal any statistically significant correlations. In Korea, sectoral growth rates tend to be negatively and significantly correlated with value added per worker. In Singapore, the relationship tends to be positive. The authors downplay the Singaporean results as having been possibly the consequence of capital deepening (and hence market-driven). On the basis of these findings, the market is then declared victorious over the government.

But, alas, the analysis is meaningless. The factor proportions theory has no implication for the correlation between *growth rates* and factor intensities (as proxied by wage rates or value added per labor) across industries.[19] Given factor endowments, the theory offers a prediction as to the pattern of specialization on the basis of factor intensities of different industries. It says nothing about how this pattern will change, unless one posits a change in factor proportions as well. It may be countered that the HPAEs' reliance on trade and therefore on comparative advantage increased over time, so that what we ought to be looking for is a convergence, again over time, toward the pattern of specialization predicted by the theory. Perhaps so. But as amply demonstrated elsewhere in the report, the HPAEs greatly increased their stock of human and physical capital in the meantime as well. A priori, the net effect on the direction of structural change is ambiguous. Once again, the report's empirical analysis does not tell us much because the appropriate counterfactual is not specified.

Moreover, there is a great deal of internal inconsistency in the use made of empirical evidence in the study. Take the case of Japan. The lack of *any* statistically significant correlations between sectoral growth rates and either sectoral wages or value added per employee in *any* of the four subperiods considered (1953–1963, 1963–1973, 1973–1980, and 1980–1989) must surely be considered a resounding failure to confirm *the authors' perceptions* of factor proportions theory. So does the report conclude that the hypothesis of market-driven structural change can be rejected for Japan? Not at all:

> The regression results shown for Japan in Table A6.2 have no significant coefficients. At least a simple version of HOS [the Heckscher-Ohlin-Samuelson theorem] does not work, probably not surprisingly as Japan by the earliest year considered in the table, 1953, was sufficiently advanced so that intra-industry rather than interindustry trade would have become an important determinant of the sectoral production structure. (p. 333)

In other words, the empirical analysis was inappropriate to begin with! One wonders what the point of running regressions is if any result will be taken to confirm the authors' priors.[20] In any case, the comment about intra-industry trade is not quite right: even as late as 1990, only 58 percent of Japan's trade was intra-industry in nature, considerably below the level in other advanced industrial countries.[21] Japan's trade would have hardly become so contentious had intra-industry trade been already dominant by 1953, as the report claims.

DID INDUSTRIAL POLICY ENHANCE PRODUCTIVITY CHANGE?

In answering this question, the report compares increases in total factor productivity (TFP) in "promoted" sectors (again at the two-digit level) with increases in TFP in other sectors. According to this test, there is evidence in favor of industrial promotion policies only in the cases of chemicals and metalworking machinery in Japan (between 1960 and 1979). Other cases do not pass the test. In Korea, there was slow TFP growth in iron and steel (a "promoted" industry) and rapid TFP growth in textiles and clothing (which was "not promoted"). In Taiwan and Malaysia, there is no apparent relationship between a sector's promotion or nonpromotion and its relative rate of TFP growth (pp. 315–16). Hence industrial policies must have been largely ineffective in fostering productivity change as well.

What is wrong with this argument? Let us review for a moment the basic economics of selective promotion. From an efficiency standpoint, the only legitimate ground for promoting certain industries over others is that the promoted industries are a source of technological externalities— benefits from technological innovation that spill over from the innovating firm to other firms or sectors. These externalities can take many forms, but let us focus, in the spirit of the report's analysis, on those that relate to TFP. To be as favorable to the report as possible, let us further grant that the spillovers remain within two-digit industries, rather than enhancing productivity in other sectors or in the economy as a whole.[22] Then a necessary (but not sufficient) condition for selective promotion to have been desirable is that the *level* of TFP must have increased as a consequence of the intervention, *relative to what it would have been* in its absence. Hence, not only is an increase in the rate of growth of TFP not required, but more important, the TFP performance of other industries is irrelevant to the desirability of the intervention. The relevant benchmark is what the TFP performance of the promoted industry itself would have been in the absence of intervention.

So consider the case of iron and steel in Korea, where TFP increased at an annual rate of 3.7 percent, compared with an industry average of 8.8 percent (Table 6.16, p. 307).[23] Now suppose, just to make the point, that TFP would have increased at a rate of 3.0 percent had promotion policies not been in effect. Then, provided the by-product costs of the interventions were small, the promotion policies would have to be judged a success. The fact that at the same time productivity increased at rates of 13.4 percent, 10.7 percent, and 12.6 percent in such technologically unrelated industries as tobacco, textiles, and leather, respectively, has no bearing on the issue at hand. If a benchmark is sought, the comparative performance of the iron and steel industries in other developing countries would perhaps provide a more accurate (but still problematic) counterfactual than the TFP performance of other sectors in Korea. Alternatively, a systematic analysis of changes in sectoral TFP performance across subperiods that differ in terms of promotion policies could have been undertaken.

Recent work by Jong-Wha Lee (not cited in the report) shows that it is possible to do more serious work along these lines.[24] Lee first constructs *direct* measures of industrial policy, such as tariffs and quantitative restrictions on imports, directed credit, and tax incentives at the sectoral level. He then uses these indicators in a panel data set of 38 Korean manufacturing industries over four five-year subperiods (covering 1963–1983) to ascertain the relationship between productivity change and government policy. The results are intriguing. He finds that trade restrictions and subsidized credit had adverse effects on TFP growth—a result at variance with the report's favorable conclusions on directed credit policies. Lee also finds, however, that tax incentives had positive effects on productivity change.[25] These results bear close scrutiny, as they do not lend themselves to any simple interpretation regarding the effectiveness of industrial policies. Moreover, Lee's paper is not entirely free of the problem of specifying an appropriate counterfactual. But the focus on direct measures of interventions and on performance across different subperiods makes it a far more reliable piece of work.

To summarize, *The East Asian Miracle's* analysis of the consequences of industrial policy lacks credibility. There is little doubt that the World Bank has done a great service by acknowledging openly the range of interventions and promotion policies used by each of the countries, and by describing these in useful detail. In view of the visibility of the Bank's work, this is of tremendous importance. It will no longer be possible to claim that East Asian governments did so well because they intervened in markets so little. But for an authoritative analysis of how these interventions worked, and which of them failed, we will have to wait for another report.

. . . .

EXPORT FETISHISM

■   AS INDICATED ABOVE, THE WORLD BANK'S REPORT concludes that policy interventions were an unqualified success in one area: exports. "Export-push strategies [a euphemism surely for export subsidization] have been by far the most successful combination of fundamentals and policy interventions and hold the most promise for other developing economies" (p. 24). In fact, it is hard to read the report without sensing a certain mercantilism running through it. No government policy, it seems, could have been harmful if its aim was to expand exports. That the HPAEs' growth performance was accompanied by a phenomenal increase in exports is of course undeniable. That exports may have played a causal role in growth is also plausible. But the report is too heavy-handed in attributing a key role to what it calls "export-push strategies," and too quick in explaining away the various puzzles that the HPAEs' experience with trade raises.

There are three broad arguments in the report with respect to the role performed by exports in generating and sustaining growth. First, exports are alleged to be the source of many favorable technological spillovers to the rest of the economy. Second, it is argued that the cross-country evidence demonstrates the growth benefits of openness. Third, the use of exports as "performance standards" for firms receiving special government favors is claimed to have rendered government interventions more effective (and less costly) than they would otherwise have been. Each of these arguments may well be true. But the analysis contained in the report will not convince anyone who is not already a convert to the faith. In what follows, I take up each of these arguments and discuss their shortcomings as presented in the report.

DO EXPORTS GENERATE TECHNOLOGICAL SPILLOVERS?

The report concludes that a high growth rate of manufactured exports, which was a consequence of export-push policies of the HPAEs, led to an economy-wide increase in TFP growth. The causal link is claimed to be "an increased ability to tap world technology" (p. 317) through exports. A number of channels through which this may have taken place are discussed, but the report provides no direct evidence to support this proposition. Cross-country regressions on growth and TFP change, discussed below, *are* presented, but these do not address specific causal mechanisms and say nothing about the existence of spillovers from exports.

Nor are most of the a priori arguments convincing (pp. 317–320). For example, it is said that competitive pressures in export markets forced firms to purchase new technology embedded in imported equipment. However, the relationship between competition in product markets and technological effort is theoretically ambiguous.[26] It is argued that export orientation fostered export-oriented foreign direct investment, which in turn created spillovers for the rest of the economy. A footnote then grants that such investment has been important as a source of investment growth neither in Japan, nor in Taiwan, nor in Korea! Nor, one may add, is there much empirical evidence on spillovers from foreign direct investment.[27] A convoluted argument is offered, which largely eludes me, regarding the advantages of export orientation in obtaining access to technology licensing from abroad.[28]

The list goes on. Perhaps the most sensible argument offered (and the one actually corroborated in specific studies) is that frequent contacts with foreign customers have served as a conduit for technology transfer from abroad. But this is too thin a branch to hang such a weighty argument on. My reading of the evidence to date is that if exports have really acted as a source of technological spillovers to the rest of the economy, we do not yet understand how this occurred.

DOES THE CROSS-COUNTRY EVIDENCE SUGGEST THAT MORE-OPEN ECONOMIES GROW FASTER?

The report's empirical analysis of the relationship between exports and growth consists of running some cross-country regressions. The strategy is to enhance the basic growth regression, discussed earlier, by adding trade-related variables on the right-hand side and demonstrating that indicators of openness have a positive association with growth. Two types of indicators are used: a measure of the size of manufactured exports (relative either to GDP or to total exports) and an "openness index" constructed by David Dollar.[29] Because the first of these indicators is obviously endogenous with respect to growth (as countries grow, so does the importance of manufactured exports in output), its use is inappropriate in this context.[30] The discussion here therefore focuses on the results obtained with the Dollar index.

Because this index has been widely abused, not least in this report, it is worth a close look. The Dollar index is essentially a measure of real exchange-rate divergence. Its links to openness, as economists understand the term (the ratio of trade to GDP, or the presence of import or export restrictions), are tenuous. An increase in trade restrictions can in fact move the Dollar index in *either* direction. These points are discussed at greater length in the appendix to this paper.

That the Dollar index lacks credibility as a measure of openness can perhaps best be seen by looking at how the index ranks specific countries (Table 5). According to Dollar's distortion index, Japan's and Taiwan's economies were more "closed" during 1976–1985 than those of Argentina, Brazil, India, Mexico, the Philippines, or Turkey! Korea's economy was more "closed" than those of any of the comparators' just named save for Argentina! The report does not highlight these results because doing so would mean giving up either on the usefulness of the Dollar index or on the claim that the HPAEs were more open than some of these leading import-substituting countries.[31]

Table 6 displays cross-country growth regressions in which the Dollar index is included as a regressor. The analysis here uses the same basic framework as that in Table 6.17 of the report, but excludes the two endogenous regressors, investment and population growth. The first column reports the result of introducing the Dollar real exchange-rate (RER) distortion index (which, as mentioned above, the report calls an openness index). The coefficient is negative and statistically significant, as in the report. The second column adds Dollar's variability index, which consists of the coefficient of variation of the RER distortion index (the coefficient of variation is simply the standard deviation of the index divided by the mean). The variability index enters significantly and renders the RER distortion index insignificant. The next two regressions combine the two Dollar indices with *direct* measures of exchange-rate policy: the average black market premium for foreign currency and its standard deviation. Both of these measures are strongly and negatively associated with growth; further, when either one of these measures is included, the Dollar indices are no longer statistically significant. Finally, when the

TABLE 5. DOLLAR INDEXES OF REAL EXCHANGE-RATE DISTORTIONS AND VARIABILITY FOR HPAEs AND SELECTED COMPARATOR COUNTRIES, 1976–1985

Economy	Distortion Index	Variability Index
HPAEs		
Hong Kong	64	0.16
Indonesia	98	0.15
Japan	118	0.09
Korea	110	0.04
Malaysia	88	0.08
Singapore	87	0.10
Taiwan	116	0.07
Thailand	75	0.07
Unweighted average	95	0.10
COMPARATORS		
Argentina	113	0.23
Brazil	97	0.13
Egypt	168	0.27
India	94	0.13
Kenya	131	0.04
Mexico	71	0.12
Philippines	92	0.13
Turkey	99	0.13
Unweighted average	108	0.15

Source: David Dollar, "Outward-Oriented Developing Economies Really Do Grow More Rapidly; Evidence from 95 LDCs, 1976–1985," Economic Development and Cultural Change, April 1992, pp. 523–544.

Gini coefficient for land distribution, used earlier, is included, the black market premia become insignificant as well. However, in this last case, the sample size shrinks to 27 countries, so the results are not particularly reliable.

Thus, what the previous discussion and the results in Table 6 show is that it is primarily exchange-rate mismanagement that appears to be harmful to growth. To the extent that there is a lesson here, it is that overvalued currencies are detrimental to long-run economic performance. From evidence presented in the report, we cannot conclude anything about the consequences of trade restrictions or of openness proper.[32]

Independent Variable	N = 103	N = 103	N = 68	N = 69	N = 27
Dollar Distortion Index	−0.0091** (−2.25)	−0.0065 (−1.59)	−0.0077 (−1.64)	−0.0078 (−1.64)	−0.0010 (−0.09)
Dollar Variability Index		−3.9830** (−2.52)	0.3673 (0.18)	1.1839 (0.57)	
Black Market Premium			−0.0084* (−2.81)		
Standard Deviation of Black Market Premium				−0.0068* (−3.26)	−0.0007 (−0.08)
Gini Coefficient for Land Ownership					4.6590** (−2.33)
Adjusted R^2	0.41	0.44	0.46	0.48	0.40

Notes: The independent variable is growth rate over 1960–1985. Each regression has the following additional regressors, the coefficients of which are not reported: an intercept, initial per capita GDP level (1960), primary enrollment ratio (1960), and secondary enrollment ratio (1960). N = number of observations. The numbers in parentheses are t-statistics. Asterisks denote levels of statistical significance; * = Significant at the 1 percent confidence level; ** = Significant at the 5 percent confidence level.

Sources: The black market exchange rate variables come from Pick's Currency Yearbook, various years (as reported by Pritchett, 1991), and cover averages for 1960–1989. The Gini coefficient for land ownership is from C.L. Taylor and M.C. Hudson, World Handbook of Political and Social Indicators, 2nd edition. (New Haven, CT: Yale University Press, 1972) and is measured around 1960.

In the context of HPAEs, there is indeed an equally plausible claim that the link between trade orientation and innovation may have gone in the opposite direction. An authoritative study on Japan's innovation system concludes that import restrictions were the most significant and helpful industrial policy in terms of stimulating research and development (R&D) effort:

> The restriction on imports and foreign direct investment into Japan was probably the most important policy until the early 1970s [as regards innovation]. Restricting the growing Japanese market, already the second largest in the capitalist economy in the late 1960s, to Japanese firms who were competing intensively among themselves gave a strong incentive to invest in plants, equipment, and R&D. In addition, because postwar Japan's Peace Constitution meant that the military was no longer a significant customer to businesses, industries such as automobiles, which had been helped by military procurement before the war but was still in its infancy relative to American and European producers, might have been wiped out were the market made open to foreign competition.[33]

Although the logic of this argument may be faulted, it is no more or less appealing than the unsatisfactory account in the World Bank report as to how export orientation promoted innovation. One is led to conclude that the jury remains out, and that there is considerable more work to do on this front.[34]

EXPORTS AS A PERFORMANCE STANDARD: DO THEY IMPROVE POLICYMAKING?

The third main avenue by which export orientation is alleged to have been conducive to superior economic performance is in improving the quality of policymaking, and of policy interventions in particular. The argument is as follows. Industrial policy entailed providing various rewards to enterprises, in return for which enterprises were expected to "perform" (that is, increase output, enhance efficiency, become more competitive, etc.). The imposition of clear performance standards in exchange for government-dispensed rewards enabled industrial policy to become effective, or at least limited its harm. It was exports that often served as the explicit or implicit performance requirement. Exports provided a clear yardstick of success, which could be used to monitor whether firms were living up to their side of the bargain.

This argument essentially merges Amsden's focus on performance requirements with the report's emphasis on exports.[35] Two questions need to be asked. First, in what sense do exports provide a superior performance standard over any other enterprise decision that can be monitored with equal ease, such as output, employment, or net foreign exchange use. Second, is there anything special about the use of performance standards in the HPAEs?

On the first question, we get only minimal help from the report:

Using exports as a performance yardstick generated substantial economic benefits. A firm's success in the export market is a good indicator of economic efficiency—a much better indicator, in fact, than success in a domestic market. Export markets are likely to be much more competitive than domestic markets. (p. 98)

To buttress its case, the report then mentions spillovers from export activities, which I have already discussed. There is actually very little in all this about the superiority of exports as a performance standard per se. The logic seems to be simply that exports generate greater economic benefit at the margin than does selling in the home market. But if that is so, surely exports ought to be encouraged for their own sake, and their use as performance standards only confuses the issues. Moreover, this emphasis on exports as a benchmark of efficiency is completely belied by a discussion shortly thereafter on how domestic commercial banks have typically preferred lending for domestic activities to lending for foreign activities (p. 99). One would have thought that rational bank managers would have used export activities as a simple screening device to distinguish more efficient borrowers from less efficient ones, if indeed the maintained hypothesis is correct.[36]

With regard to the use of performance standards more broadly, the report adopts too uncritically Amsden's argument that the use of such standards distinguishes HPAEs from other developing countries. In reality, what distinguishes HPAEs from others is the *successful* use of performance standards, which, as we shall see, is a rather different point.

Consider the firm-specific export targets used in Korea in return for the generous benefits offered to exporters during the 1960s and 1970s.

A superficial reading of the evidence would be that these targets (which were in effect performance standards) ensured good behavior on the part of the firms, and therefore prevented the subsidies from going to waste. But surely more countries must have landed on such a simple idea. And indeed they have. Performance standards of this kind are in fact not uncommon in many parts of the developing world. Some go under the less reputable name of "performance requirements" when applied to subsidiaries of multinational corporations, and are held in scorn by virtually every neoclassical trade economist.[37] Others, however, apply to domestic firms as well. In Turkey, for example, the provision of export subsidies during the 1980s was contingent on undertaking a specific quantitative export commitment.[38] In President Alan Garcia's Peru (1985–1990), the government entered into specific contracts with major exporting firms, under which advantageous exchange rates were granted to firms in return for meeting export targets.[39]

What distinguishes these cases of performance standards from the East Asian cases is the inability of governments like the Turkish and Peruvian ones to *implement* the standards. In Turkey, the export requirement was in practice easily waived: according to Krueger and Aktan, "If for some reason, the export was not realized, [the firms] simply notified [the relevant government agency] that they would not be exporting that amount, and there was no penalty."[40] In other words, the government's threat to withhold support if the firms did not live up to their side of the bargain was not a credible one. The East Asian governments, by contrast, were somehow able to make credible threats. There was a clear understanding on the part of firms in Korea that below-target performance would bring forth penalties in the form of more rigorous than usual tax inspection and tax collection.[41]   The real puzzle, then, lies with the HPAEs' singular ability to extract performance from enterprises by credibly threatening reprisal, not the presence of performance standards per se. This naturally leads us to consider issues of governance, which is the subject of the next section.

First, however, let us return briefly to the report's approving focus on export-push strategies. The report lists four elements that it says play key roles in a successful export push: exporters' access to imports at world prices, exporters' access to long- and short-term financing, government assistance in penetrating foreign markets, and flexibility in policy implementation (p. 143). The last of these is presumably a good thing under nearly all circumstances.[42] But the desirability of the first three policies, which the report recommends wholeheartedly to all countries, is predicated on the social marginal return to exports being greater than the social marginal return to production for the home market. Otherwise all producers, not just exporters, should have access to inputs at world prices, receive short- and long-term financing, and be provided with government assistance in marketing regardless of destination of output. Interestingly, the report downplays the major, generic reason why the social return to exporting may be high: the existence of import protection that biases incentives away from trade. The presence of spillovers and technological externalities from export activities, on which the report relies instead, remains no more than an article of faith.

My criticisms of the report should not be read as a rejection of the use of export-oriented policies. As I suggested at the outset, it is indeed plausible that exports were causally related to the growth performance of the HPAEs. But the objective of good economic analysis should be to uncover the precise cause-and-effect links, and to fashion policy recommendations on the basis of these links. The World Bank report falls short in that it accepts too uncritically the importance of some vague, generalized spillovers from export activities, on the basis of very little evidence.

. . . .
GOVERNANCE

■ *THE EAST ASIAN MIRACLE* RECOGNIZES that there is something special about the style of governance in HPAEs. How else can one account for the fact that policy interventions have been kept at reasonably manageable levels (in terms of both scope and magnitude) and that they have not resulted in generalized rent seeking as in so many other developing countries? The report wisely devotes the better part of a chapter (chapter 4) to a discussion of how HPAEs were able to create government capabilities that have been lacking elsewhere.

The report stresses, along with the literature, two critical aspects of the governance structure in HPAEs.[43] The first is the insulation of a technocratic elite, entrusted with the conduct of economic policy, from the push and pull of politics. Even in Indonesia and Thailand, where clientelism has been predominant, key decisionmaking structures (particularly in macroeconomic policy) have been insulated from pressures from below and sideways. This insulation is attributed partly to clever institutional design (e.g., centralization of key policy functions in independent bureaucratic organizations), partly to a willingness to distribute the fruits of growth widely, and partly to the presence of a reputable, honest civil service (achieved through merit-based recruitment and promotion, competitive remuneration, and generous rewards to those who make it to the top). But technocratic insulation can also lead to indifference to economic outcomes. So the second critical aspect is the creation of institutions ("deliberation councils" in the report's terminology) that enable communication and cooperation between the public and private sectors (particularly with business elites).

It is a plausible hypothesis that these elements, shared broadly among the HPAEs, helped create a superior governance structure. The report does a nice job of describing how each one of these elements operated in different countries. But description is not explanation. A careful reader of chapter 4 will encounter the *post hoc, ergo propter hoc* fallacy more than once. For the most part, the report ignores the obvious fact that many of the same elements have been present in other, less successful countries as well. Deliberation councils have been used widely, but too often they have served the purpose of imposing the government's policies on a reluctant private sector (as indeed has been the case at least in Korea as well). Many former British colonies have inherited a highly professional civil service: for example, it would be hard to find a more merit-based, more professional institution than the Indian Administrative Service, entry to which is even more selective than to Tokyo University. Nor do the HPAEs have a monopoly in centralized policymaking. Finally, as I will argue below, the level of corruption in many of the HPAEs is comparable to that in the rest of the developing world.

The point in raising these objections is to suggest that our understanding of the fundamental determinants of the HPAEs' governance structure is considerably more limited than what the report would lead us to believe. This point can be highlighted by focusing on two puzzles that the report sidesteps. The first has to do with the fact that the HPAEs' style of policymaking has been in fundamental conflict with economists' (and the World Bank's own) rules of good conduct. The second is related to the extent of corruption in HPAEs.

Ask any policy-oriented economist what a good policy regime should look like, and you are likely to get an answer of the following form.[44] Successful programs are likely to:

- apply simple and uniform rules, rather then selective and differentiated ones;
- endow bureaucrats with few discretionary powers;
- contain safeguards against frequent, unpredictable alteration of the rules;
- keep firms and other organized interests at arm's length from the policy formulation and implementation process.

These notions derive from various bits and pieces of economic theory, including the theories of dynamic inconsistency in policy, investment under irreversibilities, and rent seeking. The World Bank's policy recommendations, particularly in the area of trade policy, rely heavily on these or similar ideas.

The puzzle with respect to the HPAEs is that their policymaking style has been virtually orthogonal to those in the above list. Many of the interventions have been firm-specific, highly complex, and nonuniform; bureaucrats have been endowed with a tremendous amount of discretion in applying policy; rules have been changed often and unpredictably; and government officials have interacted closely with enterprise managers. *The East Asian Miracle* is filled with examples of these, but the authors succeed in putting the best face on them. Hence bureaucratic discretion and the ability to revise rules at a moment's notice become the highly desirable "pragmatism and flexibility" (p. 102) extolled throughout the report. The close interaction with firms becomes part of the "deliberation councils" idea. The reader is left puzzled as to how the HPAEs were able to strike just the right balance between opposing forces in each of these instances.

With regard to corruption, the report perpetuates the misconception that the HPAEs were blessed with relatively incorruptible bureaucracies (p. 102). This must come as a surprise to even a casual reader of the newspapers and the business press. Corruption has figured prominently as a key issue in recent election campaigns in Japan, Korea, and Taiwan alike. *The Economist* recently called Taiwan "a country where corruption scandals are a dime a dozen."[45] The most outrageous recent case involved the building of a rapid transport system in Taipei, which, thanks in part to widespread corruption in awarding contracts, has now become the world's most expensive. The current Korean president, Kim Young Sam, was elected on an anticorruption plank, and since he assumed power in February 1993 a number of top government officials, military officers, bankers, and businessmen have been arrested or have resigned. Korean government agencies where corruption has been uncovered include the Seoul metropolitan government, the much-vaunted Economic Planning Board, the Ministry of Trade and Industry, the Office of National Tax Administration, the Finance Ministry, the Seoul Subway Corporation and the Education Ministry.[46] According to the *Wall Street Journal*, corruption was "almost routine" in Hong Kong prior to 1974 (at which time an Independent Commission Against Corruption was set up).[47] Top officials of the Hong Kong Stock Exchange were arrested in 1988 in connection with irregularities during the October 1987 stock market crash.

In Thailand, the current prime minister has been identified by the *Far Eastern Economic Review* as the first elected figure in the country's history "who is tainted by neither corruption nor authoritarianism."[48] According to *International Management*, "one of the main problems [faced by Indonesia in attracting foreign business] is Indonesia's reputation as one of the most corrupt, bureaucratic, and expensive places to do business."[49] In the words of *Fortune* magazine, "To companies with high ethical standards, East Asia can be disheartening."[50]

A rough quantitative feel for the relative significance of corruption in different countries can be obtained from Table 7. The table shows the number of newspaper stories in the U.S. press since 1989 that relate to corruption in the eight HPAEs and in eight comparator countries. Japan tops the list with no fewer than 392 stories, far ahead of the next two countries, Brazil (217 stories) and Mexico (138 stories). Korea was the

TABLE 7. NUMBER OF U.S. NEWSPAPER STORIES ABOUT CORRUPTION IN HPAEs AND SELECTED COMPARATOR COUNTRIES DURING 1989–1993

Economy	Number of Stories
HPAEs	
Hong Kong	14
Indonesia	6
Japan	392
Korea	57
Malaysia	2
Singapore	4
Taiwan	6
Thailand	27
COMPARATORS	
Argentia	34
Brazil	217
Egypt	8
India	64
Kenya	37
Mexico	138
Philippines	91
Turkey	3

Source: Obtained from the NewsAbs data base covering U.S. newspapers, by doing a keyword search under "corruption [country name]."

subject of 57 stories and Thailand 27. These numbers are of course only indicative, as the U.S. media do not cover each of these countries equally. (There have certainly been more than three cases of major corruption in Turkey since 1989.) Nonetheless, the results are instructive in dispelling the notion of "relative lack of corruptibility of the public administrations in Japan and Korea" (p. 102).

This is surely yet another puzzle for which we do not have a good explanation. One qualitative difference seems to be that corruption in HPAEs has been limited to the very top echelons of the bureaucracy, whereas in many other developing countries it runs all the way down to the lowest ranks. If so, one hypothesis worth exploring is that corruption at the very top does not do nearly as much harm to economic performance as corruption at the very bottom. Why should this be so?

Shleifer and Vishny provide one plausible reason.[51] Compare the situation of a would-be importer in two kinds of bureaucratic environments. In the first, all the importer has to do is bribe a high-ranking official in the ministry of trade to obtain an import license, after which he encounters no further bribe seekers. In the second, the importer does not have to bribe any high officials, but instead must bribe a chain of low-ranking bureaucrats ranging from the doorman at the central bank, to the clerk who processes the foreign exchange application, to the customs officer on duty the day the shipment arrives. Without question, the entrepreneur would rather deal with the first type of bureaucracy than the second. As the number of officials that need to be bribed increases, so do the hassles, and so does the likelihood that the chain may be broken by some accident or another.

But there is a more subtle economic reason as well, which Shleifer and Vishny also identify. The case where a multitude of bribe seekers have monopoly power over complementary services (a foreign exchange license, an import certificate, etc.) is analogous to the double-marginalization (more accurately in this context, the multiple-marginalization) problem in industrial organization in which monopoly distortions are magnified by each distortion being built on previous ones. In contrast, a single high-ranking official would be in a position to internalize these distortions, at much lower cost to the entrepreneur and to society at large.

· ·
CONCLUSIONS

■ ONE OF THE MOST USEFUL FEATURES OF THE REPORT is its documentation of the variety of policies and institutions that comprise "the East Asian model." The model encompasses highly interventionist strategies (Japan and Korea) as well as noninterventionist ones (Hong Kong and Thailand); explicitly redistributive policies (Malaysia) as well as distributionally neutral ones (most of the rest); clientelism (Indonesia and Thailand) as well as strong, autonomous states (Korea, Japan, Singapore); emphasis on large conglomerates (Korea) as well as on small, entrepreneurial firms (Taiwan). This range of strategies, all followed more or less successfully, suggests that the search for a parsimonious explanation of the East Asian miracle may well be futile.

On the other hand, we do have a short list of initial conditions and policies that made a difference. We know that both the initial levels of schooling and the subsequent focus on education were important. We know that relative equality at the outset in terms of income and wealth must have mattered, although exactly how it mattered is not so clear. We know that macroeconomic stability, in the form of conservative fiscal policies and realistic exchange-rate management, was critical. We also know that a competent bureaucracy must have played a role. These may well account for how, in each of the HPAEs, the pieces somehow fell into place, even though the pieces themselves varied from country to country.

But, as I have argued throughout this essay, there is also plenty that we do not understand about the experience of the HPAEs. The World Bank's attempt to fit the East Asian experience into a "market-friendly" mold is only partly successful. Few would seriously disagree with the importance of macroeconomic stability and human capital formation (the first two elements of the market-friendly approach), but there are still open questions about what constitutes an appropriate approach to "openness to trade" (the third element) and "an environment that encourages private investment and competition" (the final element). Whether export orientation generates spillovers and productivity benefits beyond its obvious advantage of countering the adverse (static) effects of high import protection is still unclear. We are far from having a complete picture of what made East Asian governance structures so conducive to equitable growth. Consequently, the "correct" balance between laissez faire and intervention remains as elusive as ever.

In sum, the World Bank's report poses too few questions and provides too many easy but misleading answers. It does not acknowledge ignorance often enough.

. . . .
APPENDIX: WHAT DOES THE DOLLAR INDEX MEASURE?

■   THE DOLLAR INDEX OF "OPENNESS" is essentially a measure of the economy's price level in tradables relative to the U.S. or the world average. The starting point is the Summers-Heston price index of a comparable basket of consumption goods across countries. Because this basket includes nontradables as well as tradables, one needs to purge the effect of cross-country differences in the relative price of nontradables. As the relative prices of nontradables tend to be lower in poorer countries, Dollar accomplishes this by regressing the price index on per capita GDP (as well as its square, and on dummies for Africa and Latin America in some specifications).[52] Residuals from the regression are then interpreted as measures of the degree to which tradables prices deviate in any given country from the cross-country average.

In the published version of the paper, Dollar sensibly calls the resulting index an index of real exchange-rate distortion (calling it an index of real exchange-rate *divergence* would have been even better).[53] The World Bank report, however, calls it an index of openness. This is misleading on two counts.

First, as any student of trade theory knows, policies that affect the openness of an economy (the share of trade in GDP) do so by altering the internal relative prices of importables to exportables. Hence the appropriate measure of openness is the degree to which this particular relative price, *between* two categories of tradables, differs from the international benchmark. The aggregate price of tradables, relative to other countries', has no direct connection with the conceptually appropriate measure. To see this, consider two trade-restricting policies that (thanks to the Lerner symmetry theorem) have identical consequences for resource allocation and for openness in the long run: an import tariff of x percent, and an export tax of x percent. The first of these policies will *raise* the domestic price of tradables as a whole, whereas the second will *reduce* it (in both cases relative to the aggregate prices of tradables abroad). Judging by the Dollar index, the country restricting trade through export taxation will appear as if it has just become more open.[54]

Second, the index takes the law of one price a bit too seriously. If the experience with floating exchange rates has taught us something, it is that changes in nominal exchange rates can result in sustained movements in real exchange rates. Indeed, the nominal and real exchange rates of the U.S. dollar, to take only the most prominent case, have been almost perfectly correlated with each other since 1973. The significance of this for the Dollar index is that the movements in the index are likely to be dominated in practice by exchange-rate policy, rather than by commercial policy.[55] In other words, countries with competitive currencies (and hence low prices for domestically produced tradables) will be judged to be open by the Dollar index, whereas countries with overvalued currencies will be judged closed.

N o t e s

The author is grateful to the CEPR MIRAGE project for financial assistance, and to Michael Bruno, Albert Fishlow, Catherine Gwin, Stephan Haggard, Howard Pack, Robert Wade, and Alwyn Young for helpful comments. None of these individuals bears any responsibility for the views expressed herein.

[1] Per capita GDP in 1960 is expressed here in absolute terms, rather than relative to the United States, however.

[2] Alwyn Young, "Lessons from the East Asian NICs: A Contrarian View," *NBER Working Papers No. 4482*, October 1993, and "The Tyranny of Numbers: Confronting the Statistical Realities of the East Asian Growth Experience," unpublished paper, Masssachusetts Institute of Technology, November 1993.

[3] The same regression works very well for the 1970–1985 period as well (with initial inequality and education now measured at or around 1970). See Alberto Alesina and Dani Rodrik, "Distributive Politics and Economic Growth," *Quarterly Journal of Economics* (forthcoming).

[4] Torsten Persson and Guido Tabellini, "Is Inequality Harmful to Growth? Theory and Evidence," unpublished paper, University of California at Berkeley, 1991; Alesina and Rodrik, op. cit.; George R. G. Clarke, "More Evidence on Income Distribution and Growth," unpublished paper, University of Rochester, 1993.

[5] Kevin Murphy, Andrei Shleifer, and Robert Vishny, "Income Distribution, Market Size, and Industrialization," *Quarterly Journal of Economics*, Vol. 104, 1989, pp. 537–564.

[6] This argument crucially relies, however, on the absence of foreign trade, or at least on foreign trade being costly.

[7] Alesina and Rodrik, op. cit.

[8] Unfortunately, their index of social and political instability covers only three of the HPAEs (Japan, Taiwan, and Thailand). Alberto Alesina and Roberto Perotti, "Income Distribution, Political Instability and Investment," *NBER Working Papers No. 4486* (Cambridge, MA: National Bureau of Economic Research), October 1993.

[9] The Malaysian government has followed explicitly redistributive policies favoring ethnic Malays. But even here the starting point was a relatively equal distribution of income and wealth (as discussed above).

[10] Felipe Larraín and Rodrigo Vergara, "Investment and Macroeconomic Adjustment: The Case of East Asia," in *Striving for Growth after Adjustment: The Role of Capital Formation*, L. Serven and A. Solimano, eds. (Washington, DC: World Bank, 1993), pp. 259–260.

[11] Jeffrey D. Sachs, "External Debt and Macroeconomic Performance in Latin2 America and East Asia," *Brookings Papers on Economic Activity*, No. 2, 1985, pp. 523–573.

[12] More recent research at the World Bank has started to correct this oversight. See in particular Nancy Birdsall, David Ross, and Richard Sabot, "Inequality and Growth Reconsidered," unpublished paper, World Bank, February 1994.

[13] On Taiwan: "Political stability benefited [from land reform] in two ways. Newly landed farmers, focused on boosting production, had little interest in radical activities. Former land-lords, as new shareholders in state enterprises, had a vested interest in the success of the Taiwanese authorities' economic program" (p. 161).

[14] The report provides no systematic information on distribution relating to the pre-takeoff period. Table A5.4 gives data on income distribution, but these do not pertain to the initial condi-tions.

[15] The report explicitly mentions that the Japanese and Korean governments directed credit to specific firms and industries, mostly in heavy and chemical industries (p. 280).

[16] The report makes much of the fact that export-push policies tended to be uniform and across the board, with no industry excepted. Even so, these policies necessarily discriminated in favor of export-oriented industries and against import-competing and nontradable-goods industries. Even within exportables, larger firms were better placed to take advantage of the incentives, which was fully in accord with the Korean government's desire to nurture large conglomerates. Furthermore, export-push policies were in practice implemented in a much more discretionary manner than the report would have us believe. This point will be dis-cussed below.

[17] Alice H. Amsden, "Why Isn't the Whole World Experimenting with the East Asian Model to Develop? Review of the World Bank's *The East Asian Miracle: Economic Growth and Public Policy*," World Development, forthcoming.

[18] Linsu Kim, "National System of Industrial Innovation: Dynamics of Capability Building in Korea," in *National Innovation Systems: A Comparative Analysis*, R. R. Nelson, ed. (New York: Oxford University Press, 1993), p. 362.

[19] Note further that while value added per worker can be taken as a proxy for capital intensity, the notion of "sectoral" wages has no meaning within the factor endowments theory. According to the theory, labor is mobile across sectors, and hence there ought to be a single, economy-wide wage.

[20] The same is done in interpreting the results for Singapore (mentioned above).

[21] C. Fred Bergsten and Marcus Noland, *Reconcilable Differences? United States–Japan Economic Conflict* (Washington, DC: Institute for International Economics, 1993), table 3.3, p. 66.

[22] The report argues that this is the empirically most plausible case (p. 326).

[23] It is worth repeating that the validity of these TFP numbers themselves is very much in doubt (see Young, op. cit.).

[24] Jong-Wha Lee, "Government Interventions and Productivity Growth in Korean Manufactur-ing Industries," unpublished paper, International Monetary Fund, October 1992.

[25] The tax incentives in question include rebates of indirect taxes for exportables, and tax holidays or investment tax credits for selected firms in key industries (mostly in the heavy and chemical industries).

[26] One of the reasons for the theoretical ambiguity is actually mentioned later in the report (note 49, p. 345) in another context: an increase in relative profitability has both an income effect and a substitution effect on entrepreneurial incentives to undertake technological effort, and the two go in opposite directions. But the issues go much deeper than that. For a discussion of the issues see Dani Rodrik, "Closing the Productivity Gap: Does Trade Liberalization Really Help?" in *Trade Policy, Industrialization, and Development*, G. K. Helleiner, ed. (Oxford: Clarendon Press, 1992).

[27] In the most careful analysis of this issue to date, Aitken and Harrison conclude from plant-level data from Venezuela that there is no evidence in favor of spillovers from foreign-owned plants. Haddad and Harrison reach a similar conclusion in a study of Morocco. Brian Aitken and Ann Harrison, "Does Proximity to Foreign Firms Induce Technology Spillovers? Evidence from Panel Data," unpublished paper, World Bank, 1992. Mona Haddad and Ann Harrison, "Are There Positive Spillovers from Direct Foreign Investment? Evidence from Panel Data for Morocco," *Journal of Development Economics*, Vol. 42, No. 1, October 1993, pp. 51–74.

[28] At least one strong argument suggests the opposite. The foreign holder of the license is much less likely to sell the license to a firm that will compete head on with it in international markets than to an import-substituting firm that produces solely for the domestic market (which the foreign firm cannot access because of trade restrictions).

[29] David Dollar, "Outward-Oriented Developing Economies Really Do Grow More Rapidly: Evidence from 95 LDCs, 1976–1985," *Economic Development and Cultural Change*, April 1992, pp. 523–544.

[30] Alwyn Young (private communication to the author) has shown that the findings with regard to the manufactured exports variables are in any case not robust. The coefficient on manufactured exports (as a share of GDP) becomes insignificant when the HPAEs are removed from the sample, indicating that the trade variable itself is acting as a proxy for HPAEs. When the initial (1960) and end-of-period (1985) shares of manufactured exports in total exports are entered separately, only the latter variable remains significant.

[31] The report actually wants to play it both ways, by citing not this openness index but Dollar's "outward orientation" index when comparing the HPAEs with other developing economies. The latter index, as discussed in the appendix to this essay, combines the real exchange-rate divergence index with a variability index, as if real exchange-rate variability were something that is inherent in "inward orientation."

[32] In addition to the cross-country regressions, the report mentions some studies at the microeconomic level that find a positive association between export orientation and productivity growth. As the more careful of these studies are quick to point out, however, no causality can be attached to correlations of this sort. In particular, firms and industries that experience fast productivity growth are naturally more likely to become successful exporters. For a review of the related literature see Dani Rodrik, "Trade and Industrial Policy Reform in Developing Countries: A Review of Recent Theory and Evidence," in *Handbook of Development Economics*, Vol. 3, J. Behrman and T. N. Srinivasan, eds. (Amsterdam: North-Holland, forthcoming).

[33] Hiroyuki Odagiri and Akira Goto, "The Japanese System of Innovation: Past, Present, and Future," in *National Innovation Systems: A Comparative Analysis*, R.R. Nelson, ed. (New York: Oxford University Press, 1993).

[34] Even the data on TFP growth are in doubt. Alwyn Young (op. cit.), for one, has argued that productivity growth in many of the HPAEs is not atypically high, once factor accumulation is taken into account. This is in contrast with the conclusion put forth in the World Bank report.

[35] Alice H. Amsden, *Asia's Next Giant: South Korea and Late Industrialization* (New York and Oxford: Oxford University Press, 1989).

[36] That they apparently have not done so is rationalized in the report by banks' inadequate knowledge of foreign markets and by the greater risks associated with export-oriented projects. It is not clear why the government is not susceptible to these same problems.

[37] These performance requirements, on exports, maximum imports, local content, and so on, are typically imposed in exchange for tax holidays or similar benefits.

[38] Branko Milanovic, "Export Incentives and Turkish Manufactured Exports, 1980–1984," *Staff Working Papers No. 768* (Washington, DC: World Bank, 1986), p. 6.

[39] Ricardo Lago, "The Illusion of Pursuing Redistribution through Macropolicy: Peru's Heterodox Experience, 1985–1990," in *The Macroeconomics of Populism in Latin America*, Rudiger Dornbusch and Sebastian Edwards, eds. (Chicago: University of Chicago Press, 1991), p. 272.

[40] Anne O. Krueger and Okan H. Aktan, *Swimming Against the Tide: Turkish Trade Reform in the 1980s* (San Francisco: ICS Press, 1992), p. 247, footnote 5.

[41] Yung Whee Rhee, Bruce Ross-Larson, and Gary Pursell, *Korea's Competitive Edge: Managing the Entry into World Markets* (Baltimore and London: Johns Hopkins University Press, 1984), p. 92.

[42] The qualifier in this sentence is due to the potential trade-off between policy flexibility and the need to make binding policy commitments in order to have the private sector behave in

the desired manner. The HPAEs have somehow managed to combine these conflicting strate-gies. For a comparison of a number of countries' experience with export subsidies, see Dani Rodrik, "Taking Trade Policy Seriously: Export Subsidization as a Case Study in Policy Effectiveness," unpublished paper, Columbia University, 1993.

[43] See, for example, Peter Evans, "The State as Problem and Solution: Predation, Embedded Autonomy, and Structural Change," in *The Politics of Adjustment*, Stephan Haggard and R. Kaufman, eds. (Princeton, NJ: Princeton University Press, 1992).

[44] This discussion draws on Rodrik, "Taking Trade Policy Seriously."

[45] *The Economist*, November 6, 1993.

[46] *Asian Business*, March 1990, pp. 52–53.

[47] *Wall Street Journal*, January 1, 1994, p. A5.

[48] *Far Eastern Economic Review*, August 5, 1993, pp. 18–19.

[49] *International Management*, Europe edition, September 1985, p. 113.

[50] *Fortune*, Fall 1989, pp. 117–122.

[51] Andrei Shleifer and Robert W. Vishny, "Corruption," *Quarterly Journal of Economics*, Vol. 108, 1993, pp. 599–618.

[52] Dollar, op. cit.

[53] Ibid., p. 526. Some of the terminology later in the paper is less sensible. Dollar combines his measure of exchange-rate distortion with a measure of the variability in it to generate what he calls a measure of "outward orientation." This is unfortunate terminology for many reasons. As explained later in the text of this review, commercial policies that govern inward and outward orientation (that is, the share of trade in GDP) have no direct links to this index. In addition, the use of a variability index is baffling. It implies that inward-oriented countries have chosen, as a matter of policy, to experience more variability in their real exchange rates. The World Bank report uses this outward orientation index uncritically to argue that HPAEs were on average more open to international trade than other developing countries (p. 301).

[54] Interestingly, the report commits a Freudian slip on two separate occasions by referring to the Dollar index inaccurately: on p. 338 the index is said to measure "the correspondence between domestic and international relative prices", and on p. 301 the index is said to show that "East Asia's relative prices of traded goods were closer on average to international prices than other developing areas" (emphases added). Both of these statements are wrong. Had they been correct, the Dollar index would have been an appropriate measure of openness indeed.

[55] Dollar (op. cit.) seems to be aware of the problem, but he argues that by taking a 10-year average one can minimize the effects of year-to-year variations in real exchange rates. However, sustained misalignments of four to five years' duration are not uncommon, certainly in the developing world. Consider Chile between 1979 and 1982, Mexico since 1987, or Côte d'Ivoire since 1980, for example. In none of these cases was the real appreciation or depreciation of the currency associated predominantly with changes in trade protection.

Chapter 2

Selective Industrial Policies in East Asia: Is *The East Asian Miracle* Right?

Robert Wade

THE WORLD BANK'S STUDY, *The East Asian Miracle*, can be read as an attempt to find a compromise to a conflict of basic principles. On the one hand are the principles of the self-adjusting market and the "level playing field" that the World Bank has endorsed over the course of the 1980s and since. These principles reflect the Anglo-American belief (which is also that of mainstream economics) in a state whose role in the economy is limited mainly to providing an appropriate framework for private economic activity, and in a financial system based on private capital markets. That belief was fortified over the 1980s by the newfound power of the owners and managers of global financial capital. Their ideology says that only one set of rules should apply to all participants in the international economy, and that those rules should express a minimalist role of the state.

On the other hand are the principles endorsed by the Japanese government, reflecting Japan's own experience of a developmental state and a state-controlled, bank-based financial system. By the late 1980s Japan had begun to use its burgeoning financial muscle to transform its role in the international economic regime from that of a rule taker to that of a rule shaper, so as to change the rules to be more in line with its own demonstratedly successful system.

In response to Japanese pressure, the World Bank agreed to undertake a sustained study, funded by the Japanese government, of the East and Southeast Asian economies. The upshot of this research project, on which more than $1.2 million was spent, is that the lessons of East Asian success require virtually no modification of the Bank's recipe for development. Through the 1980s, the Bank had pressed the view that the central problem of developing countries is that they provided only a weak "enabling environment" for private-sector growth: they failed to provide adequate infrastructure, macroeconomic stability, a framework of law and property rights, transparency in policymaking, and universal primary education. *The East Asian Miracle* finds that the presence of such an enabling environment in East Asia is the main explanation of the region's superior performance. Conversely, selective industrial policies fortunately turn out to have been largely ineffective, despite the popular image of these countries as champions of industrial policy—"fortunately" because had the study found that selective industrial policies had been effective, it would have posed a serious challenge to the legitimacy of the Bank's role as intellectual leader of the debate, by seeming to undercut what the Bank had been telling the world for the past decade.

How much confidence can be placed in the report's conclusion about selective industrial policies? The conclusion is based on four kinds of arguments. The first concerns industrial structure, the second productivity growth, and the third the drive to promote heavy and chemical industries (HCI) in the Republic of Korea; and the last of the four has to do with the fast growth of the Southeast Asian countries in the absence of much "intervention."

This essay assesses these arguments in turn.[1] The conclusion drawn is that the World Bank report does not convincingly establish that selective industrial policies were unimportant for the economic success of Northeast Asia, for several reasons. First, the Bank study applies an industrial structure test, which compares the industrial structure of the East Asian economies against average industrial structure elsewhere (normalized for population and per capita income); the authors assume, wrongly, that the correspondence found between industrial structures in East Asia and cross-country averages means that these countries would have attained the averages anyway, just by virtue of free market forces. Second, the study's total factor productivity test, which compares productivity growth in promoted with those in nonpromoted industries and finds no significant difference, is substantially irrelevant and methodologically weak as well. Third, the interpretation of Korea's HCI drive is one-eyed, examining only the costs and not weighing costs against benefits. Fourth, the apparent great success of less intervention in the rapidly growing Southeast Asian economies is questionable; here the doubts relate to the basic question of whether an export-based expansion without a comparable domestic component will turn out to be sustainable.

All of these points add up to a rejection of the World Bank study's basic conclusion that selective intervention played a minimal role in East Asia's remarkable growth in the past and has no place in developing countries' policymaking in the future. There is scope for such policy, and it is not limited to Asia alone, as historical experience and some recent theoretical work suggests.

— or Britain's ! (cf Rover sale)

. . . .
THE INDUSTRIAL STRUCTURE ARGUMENT

■   THE WORLD BANK REPORT compares the manufacturing structures of Japan and Korea against Chenery-Syrquin norms, which show the shares of GDP originating in various manufacturing sectors across a cross section of countries. The conclusion: there is not much difference between the actual structures of those two countries and what the Chenery-Syrquin norms would predict.[2] The comparison is between a year in the 1960s and another in the late 1980s (Table 6.15, p. 306). This result suggests, says the report, that selective industrial policy aimed at changing the composition of industrial activity did not work, in the sense that it did not make a substantial difference from what would have happened anyway as a result of free market forces operating with reference to factor intensities and changing relative factor prices.

In the words of the report:

In Korea, for example, despite the government's extensive efforts to speed the private sector's shift from labor-intensive to capital- and technology-intensive industries, the relatively labor-intensive [and non-promoted] textiles and garments sector was nearly three times bigger than international norms predicted in 1988, a substantial increase relative to international norms from 1968. During the same period, Korea merely maintained the international norm in chemicals, a heavily promoted sector; while other heavily promoted sectors, basic metals and metal products and machinery, achieved only modest improvements. (pp. 312–13)

What is wrong with this argument? First, Chenery-Syrquin norms are based on averages across many countries, including such interventionist ones as India, Brazil, and Argentina. Therefore, it is a non sequitur to say that they show what structural changes a "normal" economy would experience in response only to free market forces—that is, in the absence of selective industrial policies.

Second, it begs two questions to say that, as their per capita incomes rose, the East Asian countries would have experienced the same structural changes without selective promotion policies. The first begged question is whether per capita income would have risen at the same speed without the selective promotion policies. The second is whether they would have been able to expand in the promoted sectors as much as they did (thus matching the Chenery-Syrquin norms) without deliberate promotion. The report simply assumes that the answer to both questions is yes. It assumes, in other words, that a free market (perhaps boosted by non-sector-specific industrial policies, such as assistance to small enterprises and to exporters) will allow poor countries to achieve an "advanced" industrial structure in a matter of a few decades.

Proponents of selective industrial policy question these assumptions. Among other grounds for skepticism, they point to increasing returns, whether due to (static) economies of scale or to (dynamic) economies of learning-by-doing, and to benefits from new activities for which the initiators are undercompensated relative to the gain to the wider economy (so-called spillover benefits or externalities). Increasing returns and externalities cause investment in the industry to be inadequate relative to the potential social returns if the investment decisions are left entirely to private entrepreneurs and real-world private financial institutions.

The industrial policy advocates also make a powerful historical point: During the past two centuries there have been few examples of countries other than microstates achieving an advanced industrial structure without selective industrial policies.

Finally, there are certain general patterns of final demand growth and technological change (or increasing linkages in an input-output table) that occur widely among middle-income countries. For example, agriculture regularly becomes more dependent on industrial outputs. (These are the sorts of regularities that the Chenery-Syrquin norms capture.) Likewise, there are regularities in the extent to which different industries have (static) increasing returns to scale and (dynamic) learning economies. The fact of these regularities *may* mean that a laissez-faire economy will move through a sequence of changes similar to that of another whose government is more dirigiste (provided the more dirigiste one is still fairly open to international competitive pressures—as North Korea is not, but as capitalist economies with managed trade such as Japan, South Korea, and Taiwan have been).

The question, however, is how quickly the changes in industrial structure will occur in each country. Precisely because of these cross-national regularities in changes in final demand and technology, it is not difficult for well-informed government officials to identify which families of industries will next have fast demand growth and productivity growth, and which ones will have increasing (static or dynamic) returns. (Remember that we are talking of middle-income countries, not countries whose firms are on the world technology frontier.) Consequently, it is not difficult for these well-informed officials—if they are also well-intentioned—to target promotional help to accelerate entry into these sectors and ease exit from sectors with slowly growing final demand, low rates of technological change, and diminishing rather than increasing returns. A government that refuses to try to promote such industries is likely to find its own entrepreneurs excluded from them, and foreign entrepreneurs in the form of multinational corporations attracted elsewhere—to countries whose governments do make targeted incentives available. Given the cumulative nature of technological learning, failure to promote these industries is likely to put the economy on a lower growth trajectory than otherwise.

THE TOTAL FACTOR PRODUCTIVITY ARGUMENT

■   THE REPORT'S SECOND MAJOR ARGUMENT is based on a comparison of total factor productivity (TFP) growth in promoted industrial sectors against TFP growth in nonpromoted sectors, where sectors are defined according to standard international trade classifications at the *two*-digit level—that is, relatively broadly. The basic finding is that, for Korea and Taiwan, there is either no significant difference between the TFP growth rates of promoted and nonpromoted sectors, or TFP growth was actually lower in promoted industries; for Japan, TFP growth was higher in promoted industries. The report's overall conclusion is that "the evidence that industrial policy systematically promoted sectors with high productivity change is weak" (p. 316). The report further concludes that:

> attempts to determine whether high rates of TFP growth combined with rapid growth of promoted sectors can plausibly explain the very high overall rates of TFP change in manufacturing yield mostly negative results. . . . The main reasons for manufacturing's success in Japan, Korea, and Taiwan . . . lay in the high general rates of TFP growth, including those in labor-intensive, nonpromoted sectors. (p. 316)

Whereas the comparison with Chenery-Syrquin norms involves a non sequitur, the comparison of TFP growth in promoted versus nonpromoted sectors proves nothing. There are at least six different problems with the TFP argument.

THE PROBLEM OF THE IRRELEVANT COMPARATOR

The standard test of infant-industry promotion involves comparing the performance of the promoted industry in country X against the performance of the same industry in the rest of the world, not the performance of the promoted industry against that of nonpromoted industries in country X (see Dani Rodrik's discussion earlier in this volume).

TFP is calculated as a residual. Slow-growing economies automatically have low TFP growth rates—but low TFP growth rates hardly explain the slow growth. In fast-growing economies (like those in East Asia), one would expect all sectors, whether promoted or not, to have large residuals—to have high TFP growth. Therefore the fact that there is not much difference in the size of the residuals between promoted and nonpromoted sectors cannot be given much explanatory significance.

More generally, the measurement of TFP depends critically on assumptions about production functions, the choice of output measure (value added versus gross output), the use of capital stock versus flows of capital services, the quality of inputs, cyclical smoothing, the time period studied, and so on. Different assumptions yield radically different results. The Bank's TFP test is based on a Cobb-Douglas production function, which assumes a fairly large degree of substitutability of labor and capital (implying relatively efficient markets) and constant returns to scale. However, a study by Park and Kwon, using a *non*-Cobb-Douglas production function incorporating an assumption of imperfect markets and nonconstant returns to scale, finds TFP growth to have been negative.[3] Even within the set of studies that use a Cobb-Douglas function, the World Bank's estimate of TFP growth for manufacturing in Korea (8.8 percent per year) is roughly twice as high as the estimates of most of the others. Given all the uncertainties about TFP, one should at least combine its use with other indicators of performance, such as export success.

THE PROBLEM OF EXTERNALITIES

The report justifies the use of two-digit sectors as the unit of analysis partly on the grounds that positive externalities spilling over from promoted to nonpromoted sectors will be largely contained within the broader two-digit sector. Therefore, if externalities are important, they should show up at the two-digit level in the form of rapid growth of promoted sectors (that is, more rapid growth in those two-digit sectors that contain a large number of promoted subsectors than in those that do not). So, according to the report, it cannot be argued that an important part of the benefits of selective promotion are missed by examining only the specifically targeted subsectors.

What is the evidence for this crucial proposition? The report cites only one study, which examines the pattern of spillovers of research and development (R&D) in industrial economies. That study suggests that the major beneficiaries of R&D spillovers in industrial economies are closely related sectors, and often those in the same two-digit classification as the sector undertaking the R&D (see p. 324). But so what? Another important form of spillovers (which some have called "slurpovers") is more general "learning" of technological mastery, which seems to be particularly important between the users of machinery and the producers of machinery (between textiles and textile machinery, automobiles and machine tools, and chemicals and plant engineering). Raw materials and chemical processing are another linked pair. Many of these pairs cross two-digit industry categories.

Two-digit sectors are much too large for the impact of selective industrial policies to be gauged. Certainly the Northeast Asian policymakers did not target such large aggregates. This being said, however, the inadequacies of the report's treatment of externalities do highlight our severe knowledge gap on the crucial question of where external benefits fall. Without better empirical knowledge, unmeasured externalities are too easily the last refuge of industrial policy advocates.

THE PROBLEM OF INTERACTION EFFECTS

If the TFP methodology is likely to miss important external benefits of selective promotion, it is also likely to miss other benefits by not examining the effects of selective industrial promotion on exports and the role of these policies in modest financial repression. The report places central importance on the East Asian policy emphasis on exports. But it identifies the content of this emphasis only in terms of policies focused directly and generically on exports (from whatever sector). Surprisingly, it fails to consider (both in the TFP test and in the rest of the report) the impact of selective industrial policies in helping the targeted firms and industries enter export markets, and it underplays causation in the

opposite direction—from exports to the disciplining of selective industrial policies.

The report also acknowledges that "modest" financial repression
may have helped growth. But it fails to acknowledge that selective industrial policies, as part of a general accumulation strategy, themselves
helped to mobilize resources (not just to allocate them) and were themselves an integral part of the modest financial repression. In other words,
the effectiveness of modest financial repression and other credit market
interventions in Northeast Asia may have been linked to the way these
interventions were integrated with protection, technological promotion,
and the like.

THE PROBLEM OF THE TIME PERIOD

The case of Korea illustrates that the choice of time period can
be critical to the outcome of the analysis. The World Bank report presents
data on long-term TFP growth in various Korean industries for a period
that is not explicitly stated but can be presumed to be from about 1965
to 1985 (Table 6.16, p. 307). The problem is that many of the promoted
industries were not promoted until the mid-1970s (for example, semicon-
ductors, shipbuilding, and steel). And by 1985 many were still recovering
from the severe recession of the early 1980s, showing much better performance after 1985. If the period had been, for instance, 1975 to 1990, the
performance of the promoted industries would have looked much better.

THE PROBLEM WITH TEXTILES

The report makes much of the fast growth, rising share of manufacturing value added, and rapid TFP growth of the Korean textiles
industry, which the report identifies as a "nonpromoted" sector. This
industry's excellent performance despite its being treated with "benign
neglect" seems a powerful point for nonintervention. There are just two
small problems.

First, the claim that textiles was not a selectively promoted industry in Korea is false. Textiles was, in fact, one of the most heavily promoted
industries, mainly because of its foreign-exchange-earning capacity. For

example, a major promotional package was put in place for textiles in 1979, and again in 1986 (so we encounter the time period problems again).[4] This was, of course, a different kind of promotion from that involved in steel, for example, but it was promotion and rationalization nonetheless. In no sense was the sector treated with benign neglect. Taiwan also gave intensive and selective promotional help to parts of textiles in several periods from the early 1950s through to the 1980s.[5]

Second, textiles and clothing's share of value added in Korea did rise over the 1970s, but over the longer period it fell sharply from 20 percent in 1963 to 14 percent in 1989.[6] The 1970s were a blip. Indeed, some of the help to the industry was designed to let parts of it down gently.

It is not clear what one should conclude from this evidence. But it is clear that one cannot say, with the report, that Korean textiles were not promoted and performed very well, and therefore one cannot use this sector to support the argument about the ineffectiveness of selective promotion.

. . . .

KOREA'S HEAVY AND CHEMICAL INDUSTRIES DRIVE

■   THE WORLD BANK REPORT CITES KOREA'S HCI drive as a case of intensive selective promotion gone wrong. The evidence? The HCI drive had very high costs: direct financial costs in the form of subsidies, and indirect costs in the form of bad loans written off. And these promoted industries had lower rates of TFP growth than did light industries. However, the relevant criterion in evaluating the impact of the HCI drive is costs against benefits, not just costs. The report is strangely silent about benefits (see Box 6.3 of the report), which is a bit like assessing a pair of scissors by examining only one of the blades.

Korea's heavy industries grew at an average rate of 17 percent a year in 1979–1988. In the same period, Brazil's grew at 0.6 percent, Mexico's at 2.7 percent, Spain's at 2.1 percent, and Greece's at −0.8 percent. Almost all of the industries within the heavy-industry category showed dramatic improvements in their trade balances during this period.[7]

These indicators suggest, prima facie, that there were substantial benefits from the HCI drive, which should be set against the costs.

Moreover, about 60 percent of the nonperforming HCI loans were accounted for by the construction sector alone. According to Amsden and Euh, the parlous financial condition of the construction industry reflects overinvestment in the Middle East—by private firms on their own initiative.[8] It cannot be blamed on dirigisme by government bureaucrats.

Finally, Park and Kwon's comparison of TFP growth in light industries with that in HCIs yields the opposite finding from the Bank's: that the HCIs had decisively faster TFP growth than the light industries, which is roughly the same as saying that the promoted industries had faster TFP growth than the nonpromoted industries. Their conclusion holds whether one uses a standard method for calculating TFP or the nonstandard type of production function described earlier. Interestingly, it also holds for the specific sectoral contrast on which the World Bank study puts a lot of weight: whereas the Bank study says that the promoted iron and steel industry had slow TFP growth and the nonpromoted textiles and clothing industry rapid TFP growth, Park and Kwon, studying the same time periods, find exactly the opposite.

. . . .
THE SOUTHEAST ASIA ARGUMENT

■ MALAYSIA, THAILAND, AND INDONESIA— the southern tier of high-performing Asian economies—have enjoyed fast growth over the 1980s without much in the way of selective industrial policies, thanks to far-reaching liberalization during that decade. This seems to confirm that government efforts to go beyond measures to provide infrastructure and strengthen the market framework are not necessary for fast, catch-up growth.

Things are not so simple, however. The fast growth of the southern tier has probably been driven to an important extent by the industrial restructuring and fast growth of the northern tier—"probably" because there seems to be little quantitative evidence. But if one put into a growth regression a variable that captures the growth of other countries in the region, the intraregional growth effect would probably show up as important. Given the World Bank study's general appetite for growth regressions, the inattention to regional "neighborhood" effects is surprising. On the face of it, a strong neighborhood effect would qualify a central argument of the study, namely, that factors internal to each country are the prime determinants of each country's growth rate. Insofar as growth stimuli from the northern-tier countries are important, and insofar as those stimuli have been concentrated on the southern-tier countries because of their geographical and cultural proximity, the internal factors are less important than the study suggests.

We do not know much about the causal relationships involved in this neighborhood effect—to what extent it works through trade, through foreign investment, through imitation, or through overseas Chinese networks. But we do know that foreign direct investment has been a big part of the story, particularly since the massive currency realignments initiated by the Plaza Agreement in 1985. The southern-tier countries received a great wave of direct investment, first from Japan and then from Taiwan and Korea, as firms from the northern tier, facing appreciating currencies and rising labor costs at home, and rising protection in their export markets, sought production sites abroad that offered lower costs and were not yet subject to import quotas abroad.

The results of this investment so far raise some doubts about the robustness of the southern tier's future growth and about the replicability of its growth mechanism. To begin with, this foreign investment is heavily export oriented. Three-quarters or more of the output of foreign manufacturing subsidiaries in the southern-tier economies is exported. To that extent these countries' overall growth does not depend on growth in the domestic economy. The foreign investment is also concentrated in a narrowish product range—consumer electronics and other low-end electrical and electronic manufacturing.

Moreover, the exports of these foreign subsidiaries account for a very large proportion of total manufactured exports. For example, over 90 percent of Malaysia's exports of machinery, electrical appliances, and consumer electronics come from foreign-owned plants.[9]

The foreign subsidiaries rely heavily on imported inputs. They thus constitute export enclaves, with only weak backward or forward linkages to domestic firms. Local content requirements imposed by host governments are being met in large part by inputs from other foreign-owned subsidiaries rather than from domestically owned firms. For example, the local content of consumer electronics goods produced by Japanese firms in Malaysia was only 30 percent in 1988, and most of the local parts were produced by other Japanese firms in Malaysia. Malaysian-owned firms mostly supplied packing materials and simple pressed parts.[10] In automobiles the situation is even more extreme. From the standpoint of the domestic economy, this is "technologyless industrialization."[11]

These tendencies are being reinforced by the development of complex regional hierarchies of production. Some Korean and Taiwanese firms that had been producing at home for Japanese firms on an OEM (original equipment manufacturing) basis have now established plants in the southern tier.[12] They may continue to produce for Japanese firms on an OEM basis in the new plants, obtaining their capital equipment and their high-value-added components from Japan, while themselves supplying the management and lower-value-added components. The host economy provides only the labor, land, energy, and the right to pollute the environment.

The industrialization of the southern tier is therefore vulnerable to the relocation decisions of multinational firms. Because they are only weakly integrated into the local economies, the agents of southern-tier industrialization are more likely to move their operations to sites where labor is cheaper (for example, Indochina) as local costs rise. Given the previous points, this aborts the alternative response of upgrading technology in response to rising costs. The host economy's long-term growth potential is in question, because its ability to sustain continual rises in real wages (an indicator of development success) is diminished.[13]

In contrast with the northern-tier governments, those of the southern tier not only have allowed a foreign direct investment free-for-all, but also have been doing much less to forge links between foreign and domestic firms. That is to say, they have been abiding more closely by World Bank principles. They have also been doing less to improve the economy's general level of technological capacity—they have invested less in higher education and in R&D facilities, for example. This comparison is admittedly impressionistic. No sustained comparison of industrialization policy between the Northeast and Southeast Asian countries appears to have yet been made. It is a matter of regret that the World Bank study says almost nothing about it.

The growth mechanism in the southern tier is critically dependent on Japan as the supplier of capital goods, high-value-added components, technology, and aid, and on the United States as the demander of first resort. Virtually all the high-performing East Asian countries run large trade deficits with Japan and large surpluses with the United States. Indeed, the United States takes more than twice as much of Korea's and Thailand's manufactured exports as Japan does, and four to five times as much of Taiwan's and Malaysia's. Particularly striking is how little of the production of Japanese manufacturing subsidiaries in the southern tier is exported back to Japan—only 10 percent of sales in 1989. These imbalances are driving the well-known trade tensions in the region. If and when the United States reduces its balance-of-payments deficit, will Japan become a significantly larger absorber of manufactured goods from the region? On the answer to this question much of the future growth of the region depends.

What is the relevance of all this to the World Bank study's conclusion about selective industrial promotion? The study suggests that it was liberalization in the Southeast Asian cases that mattered, rather than anything to do with selective industrial policy. It further suggests that other countries could have enjoyed the benefits of fast growth had they, too, liberalized in the 1980s. The argument developed here suggests, in contrast, that the fast growth of Southeast Asia in the 1980s was a reflex of industrial restructuring in Northeast Asia (the response to which was facilitated by southern-tier liberalization of controls on inward direct investment). The fact that Northeast Asian firms moving production offshore went to Southeast Asia rather than to Latin America or South Asia may be due less to the fact that Southeast Asia had better "fundamentals" than other cheap labor sites (as the report would argue), and more to other, regionally specific factors. About these we know rather little, but they would certainly include overseas Chinese networks, similarities in business practices, and the advantages of geographical proximity (even today when the technology is available to shrink great distances).

Two important conclusions follow. First, to the extent this argument is correct, the replicability of the Southeast Asian experience is put in question. Second, the dependence of that experience on foreign direct investment, and the failure to anchor foreign firms in the domestic economy through input-output linkages, means that the continuing transformation of Southeast Asian industrialization into higher-value-added activities is also in question.

In a word, the Southeast Asian experience of fast growth without selective industrial policies does not do much to dent the argument that selective industrial policies were important in Northeast Asia, or the argument that would-be catch-up countries in other parts of the world, and in Southeast Asia itself, should consider selective industrial policies to help them move into higher-value-added activities.

. . . .
WORLD BANK ECONOMICS VERSUS EAST ASIAN ECONOMICS

■   OVERALL, ONE HAS TO CONCLUDE that the World Bank study's evidence for the proposition that selective industrial policies were ineffective in Northeast Asia is less than compelling. It also has to be said, however, that the evidence provided by the so-called revisionists about the effects of the industrial policies that they so lovingly describe is less than compelling. It leaves them open to the quip that a revisionist is someone who thinks the plural of "anecdote" is "evidence." In the end a judgment must be made about the balance of plausibility.

Two reasons can be offered to explain why the mainstream judgment has favored the view that East Asian success is due *mainly* to the fact that markets worked better there, with less government distortion. One reason is that the theoretical apparatus for the study of competitive markets is much better developed than that for analyzing state power, organizations, and imperfect competition. Another is that the mainstream is inattentive to history. One can move the debate forward by developing theoretical rationales for what East Asian policymakers actually did, and by setting the East Asian experience in a wider historical context.

The report's discussion is rooted in the Anglo-American debate over whether the government can "pick winners." This concept, and the

World Bank's TFP test itself, assume that winning sectors are identified by their profitability or productivity performance. Other characteristics, and in particular the links with other industries, are not central. If potato chip manufacturers have higher productivity growth rates and profits than semiconductor chip manufacturers, then potato chips are the winners. (Formally, one can factor in such considerations through the distinction between social and private profitability. But "social" profitability does not capture the idea of families of interconnected industries.)

The East Asian conception is different. The task is not to pick winners, but to identify "key" industries. The concept of key industries stresses links with other industries—an increasing density of input-output linkages within the domestic economy and positive spillovers from key industries to others.

This difference stems from a more fundamental difference between a "framework" approach to public policy for economic development and an "ingredients" approach.[14] In the World Bank framework approach, the attention is on correcting distortions in price signals, so that individual agents can make investment and innovation decisions that are as close to optimal as possible. There is no presumption that anyone, least of all the government, can guess with any accuracy the structure of the economy that will result from these individual decisions. Indeed, an essential feature of a good framework is that no actor can exercise any perceptible influence on the structural outcome. (This has its roots in Adam Smith's one-eyed conviction that harmful effects occur whenever power is used to alter the "natural course of economic life.")

In the (East Asian) ingredients approach, the attention is very much on the tangible structure of the economy, defined as a set of industries and organizations already in place (the ingredients), and especially on the desirable future structure of the economy. Public policies and organizations are designed so as to achieve a vision of the economy's future structure.

The difference is seen most vividly when an industry is in trouble. According to the framework approach, the government should remain indifferent about whether the industry disappears, moves offshore, pays lower wages, or upgrades its technology so that it can continue to compete at current wages. The only exceptions arise when national security considerations are involved and when competition is unfair. According to the ingredients approach, the government would be abdicating an essential responsibility if it did not have a view on the importance of the industry in its vision of the economy's future, and did not take action to produce results in line with that view.

The ingredients approach thinks in terms of stages of industrialization. Japanese postwar industrialization, for example, is often divided into a first stage of export-oriented, labor-intensive, light industrialization (textiles, household appliances) from 1950 to the late 1960s; a second stage of export-oriented heavy and chemical industrialization (steel, shipbuilding, petrochemicals, synthetic fibers) from the mid-1960s to the early 1970s and the first oil shock; a third stage of export-oriented, assembly-based, skill- and R&D-intensive consumer durables and industrial machinery from the late 1960s to the late 1980s; and a fourth stage of home-market-oriented, flexible manufacturing from the early 1980s onward. Each stage was associated with certain kinds of public policies, and each encountered certain growth constraints, which prompted the shift to the next stage. Each stage also generated characteristic forms of international trade, investment, and aid.[15]

Japanese officials and academics tend to assume that other economies in the region are traveling along the same basic path. Behind Japan come the second-tier followers, Taiwan and Korea; behind them the third tier, Malaysia, Thailand, and Indonesia; and behind them the fourth tier, China and perhaps the Philippines. Further, they tend to assume that East Asia is an interrelated economy, with industrial restructuring from one stage to another in the more advanced countries generating, through those characteristic forms of international trade, investment, and aid, growth impulses directed toward the less advanced countries.

This, put simply, is the "flying geese" theory of East Asian development. As was suggested earlier, there is plenty that is wrong with such a mechanical notion. But it seems an improvement on the "marathon" metaphor of development that underlies neoclassical thinking, according to which the relative position of each country is a function largely of its own internal resources, and in which all countries could, conceptually, be equally wealthy (all run abreast). Like it or not, the flying geese approach is certainly shaping the Japanese government's economic strategy in the region.

The content of public policy, in this view, is derived from what has to be done to prepare the way for the next stage of industrialization. Whereas the framework approach sees trade policy as the king of policies, not just one among many (because if the trade regime gives low or no protection, the government has little scope to mess up the economy with other kinds of interventions), the ingredients approach sees trade policy as subordinate to a wider industrial strategy, with technology and education policies as king and queen.[16] The decision about whether to protect an industry is made not with reference to a general belief that tariffs and import controls lower economic welfare and should be avoided in all but exceptional conditions, but with reference to how protection, as one form of assistance among others, might help to move the industry along its designated trajectory in the wider vision. It is assumed that protection and the other forms of assistance may be decisive only for some industries in some countries at some stages of their growth, not for all industries at all stages.

There is as yet not much theory behind the ingredients approach. Certainly what is called "strategic trade theory" is of little relevance to what the East Asian governments did, as the World Bank has been at pains to point out.[17] But there are several kinds of "soft" strategic intervention theory that have been developed to some extent and that do seem highly relevant. They refer to rationales for government intervention to promote selected industries for (soft) strategic reasons—not to raise the immediate profitability of the targeted industries, but to confer external benefits on other industries and to improve the competitiveness of one's own industry vis-à-vis those of competitors elsewhere. They start from the recognition that countries specialize in different industrial products less for reasons of relative factor endowments than for reasons of which country is first able to capture economies of scale and economies of learning in a given industry, and thereby (because of the resulting high entry costs) deter firms elsewhere from entering.[18]

In the case of industries with increasing returns (due to economies of scale and learning), there is no theoretical presumption that free market forces will reach an equilibrium that is not only stable but also welfare maximizing. There is indeed no general presumption that nonintervention by government will be more beneficial than selective promotion. Which of many possible stable equilibria is actually arrived at—which pattern of specialization—depends on exogenous factors, such as accidents of history and industrial policies.

And the pattern of industrial specialization at any one time tends to set the direction for future development, because much technological knowledge is specific in application ("tacit" rather than "codified") and cumulative or path-dependent in development. Under these conditions, price signals cannot be relied on to produce investment and innovation decisions that are anything close to socially optimal. They may lead entrepreneurs to specialize in low-value-added activities that face slow-growing markets. The result may be to "lock in" to a permanently lower growth trajectory than could be achieved with the same static comparative advantage where extra resources are allocated, by fiscal decision or deliberately "distorted" prices, to technological learning. By exercising economy-wide foresight, governments can foster the development of "leading" industries that "drive and mold economic progress across a broad front"[19] by generating externalities for a broad spectrum of other industries, thereby raising the future, path-dependent technological level of the economy.

This is the sort of theory that has to be developed in order to understand what the East Asian policymakers actually did. It has to be reinforced by wider historical analysis of industrialization. We have been misled by Adam Smith's thundering against mercantilist policies, and by later economists who treated mercantilism as the economic equivalent of flat-earth theory. They have failed to see that, in Smith's own day, England's economic and political superiority over France, Sweden, and even Holland resulted from the greater "coherence and rationality of [its] mercantilist economy,"[20] or that Western Europe's economic and political superiority over the rest of the world was established during the mercantilist era. Later, it was the Prussian mercantilist state that forged the economic and political unification of Germany, while nonmercantilist Poland fell apart. The Russian and Japanese states were guided by mercantilist ideas, while nonmercantilist China was brought to its knees. Indeed, in the typical case the governments of today's advanced industrial countries took measures to favor certain actors and shut others out, and to protect new industries from established competitors elsewhere. We do not well understand just how necessary such actions were in each industry in each country. Sometimes protection was maintained for a short time, and sometimes it persisted for decades; sometimes persistent protection seems to have been necessary in order to master the technology (consider, for example, the Japanese automobile industry), and in other cases it may have persisted too long, beyond the point of significant net learning benefits—although this is not to say that the bulk of the learning benefits could have been acquired with no protection at all.

These facts have not received the attention they deserve, partly because we still operate under a Smithian assumption that the unit of analysis is the individual, not the nation-state, and still foolishly confuse mercantilism à la Friedrich List with socialism. The mercantilism of Europe and East Asia is all about building "rich country, strong military," in the Meiji phrase (that is, a rich country *for* a strong military), or building an economy strong enough to provide the means to fend off external threats. Limiting international trade and granting special trading privileges were a way to foster national merchant classes, entrepreneurs, and new industries. These fostered entities in turn provided revenue to the state, allowing it to expand its military capabilities. To portray mercantilism merely as a system where vested interests pushed and pulled the state to advance their interests is seriously wrong.

This is not to suggest that all cases of economic development in Europe required a mercantilist period. Some states benefited from spillover growth stimuli from mercantilist growth centers nearby, as may be happening in Southeast Asia today. But these appear to have been exceptions. Putting the experience of the European mercantilist states together with that of the Northeast Asian developmental states of the postwar period, we have grounds for concluding that, exceptions like Hong Kong and Denmark aside, they show us, analytically, what is required for fast and sustained development to occur. In any case, the combination of the new formal economic theories and the interpretive theories of historical industrializations is making the established paradigm increasingly unattractive, and providing the shaft on which a new one will crystallize.

. . . .

THE WORLD BANK'S STANCE ON SELECTIVE INDUSTRIAL POLICIES: A MODEST CONCLUSION

■ THERE IS REASON TO WORRY whether the World Bank's refusal to countenance selective industrial policies for industries with relatively high entry barriers reflects an underlying unwillingness to help developing countries enter industries that are already well established in the West, especially when Western plants have excess capacity. Or, more exactly, the Bank's refusal to help these countries mount selective industrial policies targeted on high-entry-barrier sectors means that if these economies are to enter these sectors, it must be largely at the invitation of Western and Japanese multinationals, with the host country itself having relatively little bargaining power. Given the governance structure of the World Bank, it is not difficult to imagine why. This is quite different from the way in which the Northeast Asian countries got established in these sectors—by using intensive selective industrial policies to forge partnerships or technology agreements between domestic firms and foreign multinationals.

Of course, the Bank is right to emphasize the dangers of selective industrial policy, but *The East Asian Miracle* would have done a service by examining in detail *how* the East Asian countries integrated protection, export promotion, industrial, technology, and education policies. Some would say that it is just at this point, which the study rushes past with a few casual remarks, that the real lessons of East Asian public policy lie. Such a study would show that it is not the case, as much Bank thinking assumes, that selective industrial policy must be done either on a big scale or not at all.

Take a small example from Taiwan. The subsidiary of a multinational enterprise was producing a product in Taiwan for which it needed a certain chemical of a very high level of purity, above that reached by domestic chemical makers. It was therefore importing the needed supplies. At a certain point the official in the Industrial Development Bureau responsible for that part of the chemical sector concluded that, with a little help, one or more Taiwanese chemical companies could produce the chemical to the requisite level of purity. He contacted the importing company and some relevant Taiwanese companies to discuss the possibilities. He urged the importing company to enter into a long-term supply agreement with one or more of the Taiwanese companies and to provide them with technical help. The company declined. But it then began to find that its applications to import the chemical, which previously had been immediately approved (all imports to Taiwan, at least until the late

1980s, have had to have a license, even when automatically approved), began to be delayed, and the delays began to lengthen. Eventually the company did what the official wanted, and one more Taiwanese company was helped to upgrade its technology, thanks to the ability of the government to use its control over imports as an instrument for strengthening the national economy.[21]

This is a selective industrial policy of sorts, but it is a "low-powered" selectivity, a far cry from what is normally meant by "picking winners." It shows how selective industrial policy can be done in a small, incremental way. Governments with weak capacity can begin with selective industrial policy on a modest scale, not attempting to pick winners from a long menu, but identifying what activities already going on in the country seem to be doing well, analyzing what public policy could do (and stop doing) to foster those activities, and putting low-powered programs in place. Indeed, quite a lot of Taiwanese industrial policy was little more than an attempt to nudge existing firms to upgrade their technology—both by functional or across-the-board measures and by actions focused on "strategic" (or key) industries, as in the above case. Of course, Taiwan also used high-powered selective policies as well, when the aim was a big jump in technological capability. These included sequencing the development of new industries and limiting entry to scale-intensive industries, so as to achieve economies of scale of production capacity and cumulative technological learning, and the creation of infrastructural R&D organizations for the targeted industries.[22]

To do selective industrial policy well on the scale done in East Asia probably does require a strong, fairly authoritarian state[23] (but not necessarily a nondemocratic one: Japan has had a democracy of sorts these past fifty years). But it can be done on a much smaller scale, by a smaller bureaucracy better able to be insulated from the pressure groups of a Western-style democracy or even the personalistic networks of a patrimonial-bureaucratic state. *There is a learning effect in bureaucracy as surely as in industry.* If governments do not attempt to accelerate, even modestly, the acquisition of technological learning in important industries, they will not learn how to do so. If they do not learn to do so, their firms will be handicapped in entering these sectors. Those in the West who do not want to see new competitors in these industries—or at least new competitors not under the control of their own multinationals—may applaud this outcome. The World Bank should not.[24]

But industrial policy is not just about building new industries and managing the decline of old ones. It can also be part of a wider strategy to tame the socially destructive effects of free markets—to check the propensity of people operating in a free market ethos to see free riding as perfectly fair, and so to erode the bonds of community, tradition, and authority. Industrial policy, in other words, can be a source of social order and discipline, a means of nation building. Neither in *The East Asian Miracle* nor any of its other work has the World Bank begun to address such issues. It simply assumes that full-scale marketization in the context of what it means by the "enabling environment" is fully compatible with social order. The mercantilists knew better.

In a word, *The East Asian Miracle* makes a variety of theoretical and empirical assumptions that bias the results against selective industrial policy. On the other hand, it has given the issue more serious, less rhetorical attention than any other Bank publication in the past decade, and its arguments can be taken as an agenda for further research—whether inside the Bank or not remains to be seen.

Notes

[1] A veritable cottage industry has sprung up in assessments of *The East Asian Miracle*. The author has benefited from the following published and unpublished comments: Ha-Joon Chang, "Failures of East Asian Industrial Policy: A Comment on the World Bank's 'East Asian Miracle' Study," appendix in "Explaining 'Flexible Rigidities' in East Asia," paper for an ODI Workshop on the Nature, Significance, and Determinants of the Flexibilities of National Economy, Overseas Development Institute, London, 1993; Masaki Shiratori, "The Role of Government in Economic Development: Comments on 'East Asian Miracle' Study," and Toru Yanagihara, "Framework Approach and 'Ingredients Approach,'" papers presented to an Overseas Economic Cooperation Fund conference on The East Asian Miracle, Tokyo, 3 December 1993; John Williamson, "East Asia: Enlightenment," *International Economic Insights*, Vol. 4, No. 6, November-December 1993, pp. 35–36; David Evans, "Tests of Selective Industrial Policy," unpublished paper, Institute of Development Studies, Brighton, England, 1993; Jene Kwon, "On the 'East Asian Miracle,'" unpublished paper, Department of Economics, Northern Illinois University, De Kalb, 1993; and Sanjaya Lall, "The East Asian Miracle Study: Does the Bell Toll for Industrial Strategy?" Dwight Perkins, "Review of the World Bank's 'The East Asian Miracle,'" and Alice H. Amsden, "Why Isn't the Whole World Experimenting with the East Asian Model to Develop? Review of the World Bank's *The East Asian Miracle: Economic Growth and Public Policy*," papers presented at a Symposium on the World Bank's East Asian Miracle Report, to be published in *World Development*. See further Colin Bradford,

"From Trade-Driven Growth to Growth-Driven Trade: Reappraising the East Asian Development Experience," OECD Development Center, Paris, November 1993. The author has also benefited from the comments of the coauthors in this volume and from discussions with Lance Taylor, Devesh Kapur, Manfred Bienefeld, Hans Singer, Howard Pack, Catherine Gwin, and Peter A. Petri.

[2] Hollis Chenery and Moshe Syrquin, *Patterns of Industrial Growth, 1950–70* (New York: Oxford University Press, 1975).

[3] Seung Rok Park and Jene Kwon, "Rapid Economic Growth with Increasing Returns to Scale and Little or No Productivity Growth," unpublished paper, Northern Illinois University, De Kalb, 1993, cited in Jene Kwon, op. cit. Another problem is that the report cites a 1979 study by Dollar and Sokoloff that gives quite different rankings of industries by long-term TFP growth than the report itself does. Dollar and Sokoloff show slow TFP growth for textiles and fast TFP growth for petroleum, the opposite of the World Bank report's results.

[4] See Ha-Joon Chang, "The Political Economy of Industrial Policy in Korea," *Cambridge Journal of Economics*, Vol. 17, 1993, pp. 131–157, table 4.

[5] Robert Wade, *Governing the Market* (Princeton, NJ: Princeton University Press, 1990), chapter 4.

[6] Kwon, op. cit., table 2.

[7] Chang, op. cit., p. 135. See also Operations Evaluation Department, "World Bank Support for Industrialization in Korea, India, and Indonesia" (Washington, DC: World Bank, 1992); Rick Auty, "Industrial Policy Reform in Six Large NICs: The Resources Curse Thesis," *World Development*, Vol. 22, No. 3, January 1994; and Wade, *Governing the Market*, chapter 10.

[8] Alice H. Amsden and Yoon-Lee Euh, "Republic of Korea's Financial Reform, What Are the Lessons?" *Discussion Papers*, No. 30 (Geneva: UNCTAD, 1990), cited in Amsden, op. cit.

[9] World Bank, *Foreign Direct Investment from the Newly Industrialized Economies* (Washington, DC: World Bank, 1989).

[10] Etsuro Ishigami, "Japanese Business in ASEAN Countries: New-Industrialization or Japanization?" *IDS Bulletin*, Vol. 22, No. 2, April 1991, pp. 25–26. See also N. Yawata and J. Mizuno, "The Division of Labor Within Industries, and Technology Transfer Between Japanese Industries Abroad and Local Industries," unpublished paper, Institute of Developing Economies, Tokyo, 1990.

[11] Kunio Yoshihara, *The Rise of Ersatz Capitalism in Southeast Asia* (Singapore: Oxford University Press, 1988).

[12] Original equipment manufacturing is an arrangement whereby one company contracts with another to manufacture a specified product, which the first company then sells under its own name.

[13] This is a preliminary conclusion, which needs to be confirmed by examining microeconomic evidence on reinvestment behavior—expansion of existing plants, labor force training, and so on—in host countries by already established firms.

[14] Yanagihara, op. cit.

[15] Ozawa Terutomo, "The Dynamics of Pacific Rim Industrialization: How Mexico Can Join the Asian Flock of 'Flying Geese,'" in *Mexico's External Relations in the 1990s*, Riordan Roett, ed. (Boulder, CO: Rienner).

[16] Robert Wade, "Managing Trade: Taiwan and South Korea as Challenges to Economics and Political Science," *Comparative Politics*, Vol. 25, No. 2, 1993, pp. 147–167.

[17] Strategic trade theory shows how government action can shift rents from oligopolistic foreign to oligopolistic domestic firms, improving not only the profitability of domestic firms but also national welfare. For the World Bank position, see World Bank, "Strengthening Trade Policy Reform," November 1989, Box 1-2.

[18] For further discussion see Wade, *Governing the Market*, chapter 11. Also see Trevor Matthews and John Ravenhill, "Strategic Trade Policy: The East Asian Experience," *Working Papers*, Vol. 1993/2 (Canberra: Research School of Pacific Studies, Australian National Univer-

sity); Sanjaya Lall, op. cit.; and Martin Bell and Keith Pavitt, "Technological Accumulation and Industrial Growth: Contrasts Between Developed and Developing Countries," *Industrial and Corporate Change*, Vol. 2, No. 2, 1993, pp. 157–210.

[19] Richard Nelson, *High-Technology Policies: A Five Nation Comparison* (Washington, DC: American Enterprise Institute, 1984), p. 1.

[20] C. Wilson, *Economic History and the Historian* (London: Weidenfeldt and Nicholson, 1969), p. 153, cited in Christer Gunnarsson, "Mercantilism Old and New: A Transaction Cost Theory of Developmental States in Europe and East Asia," unpublished paper, Department of Economic History, Lund University, Lund, Sweden, 1993. The present discussion draws on this paper. The author has also benefited from Dietre Senghaas, *The European Experience* (Dover, NH: Berg, 1985) and from John Brewer, *The Sinews of Power: War, Money and the English State 1688–1783* (London: Unwin Hyman, 1989).

[21] For further discussion, see Wade, *Governing the Market, op.cit.* chapter 5.

[22] Ibid.

[23] Cf. Martin Wolf ("Paths to Progress," *Financial Times*, 15 November 1991), who says, "If the price of successful interventionism is authoritarianism, it is one that does not have to be paid.... What reforming countries need is democratic constitutions that allow [the market to work], not more interventionism."

[24] See further Wade, *Governing the Market, op.cit.* chapter 11.

Chapter 3

Politics and Institutions in the World Bank's East Asia

Stephan Haggard

■ THE WORLD BANK STUDY of *The East Asian Miracle* constitutes an impressive effort to synthesize the complex influences that have produced rapid growth in the high-performing Asian economies (HPAEs). Two features of the report stand out. The first is the finding that direct government intervention in markets contributed to rapid and equitable growth, particularly in Japan, the Republic of Korea, and Taiwan. This observation is not novel; it has been the accepted wisdom for over a decade among specialists on the region. Moreover, the report makes this concession to heterodoxy only grudgingly. The importance of policy "fundamentals" is repeated again and again, but the findings on intervention are ringed with reservations and caveats.

Nonetheless, the change in the Bank's views, however subtle, is likely to shift the debate on economic growth in a productive way. Vulgar neoclassicism—the view that East and Southeast Asia succeeded through market-oriented policies alone—will finally be relegated to the intellectual scrap heap where it belongs, clearing the way for a more productive dialogue on the complicated relationship between states and markets in Asia.

Because Dani Rodrik and Robert Wade address this controversy eleswhere in this volume, this essay will focus on a second but equally important contribution of the report: the emphasis on institutions, including political institutions, in the development process.[1] The implication of *The East Asian Miracle* is not only that the HPAEs got their policies "right," but that they got their institutions and even their politics "right" as well. This line of inquiry is much riskier than the analysis of policy per se. Difficult as it may be to convince unwilling governments to change policies, it is even more demanding to develop efficient institutions or to rearrange political systems so that they generate and sustain growth-promoting policies. It is also highly debatable whether the HPAEs present us with political models worthy of being emulated, even if they could be.

Although the focus on the political economy of growth is hardly new, much of what the report says about institutions and politics is on target. The discussions of labor policy, business-government relations, and the significance of bureaucratic insulation are all refreshingly frank. There are also some intriguing theoretical ideas in the report, particularly the idea of creating "contests" in order to limit the capture of policy by rent-seeking groups.

Despite these contributions, there are also limitations in the report's institutional and political analysis. These limitations spring in part from political constraints on the World Bank as a multilateral institution. Despite the report's generally candid tone, some thorny political issues, such as the relationship between authoritarianism and rapid growth in the HPAEs, are treated gingerly. Other problems spring from a fundamental ambivalence about the utility of government intervention and a hesitation to draw firm conclusions about institutional design or political strategy, even where the evidence appears to warrant such conclusions.

This essay begins with a discussion of initial conditions in the HPAEs, focusing on their sociological inheritance. This inheritance was profoundly different from that of the developing countries with which the HPAEs are typically compared. In particular, the HPAEs did not have large landowner classes. As a result, the distribution of both income and assets was relatively equitable *prior* to the adoption of export-oriented policies. These initial conditions contributed to subsequent economic performance, suggesting the importance of equity as an "input" to growth.

Although the World Bank's report seeks to outline the policies that contributed to rapid growth in East and Southeast Asia, it does not address the question of why these policies were adopted in the first place; accordingly, the second section of this essay addresses this problem of the political economy of policy reform. Not surprisingly, economic crises were typically a triggering factor. Yet what is striking about the HPAEs' experience is that the crises were exploited by political elites, who concentrated political authority while simultaneously delegating power to insulated technocratic agencies. Strong states were a crucial prerequisite for reform, important not only in guaranteeing the relative efficiency of interventions at the microeconomic level, as the report emphasizes, but for the coherence of economic policy more generally.

It is one thing to initiate reforms; it is another to sustain them over time. As the report rightly emphasizes, sustaining reforms demands the construction of bases of political support. The third and fourth sections of this essay examine the World Bank's interpretation of how the HPAEs did this.

The report's emphasis on the importance of "shared growth"—the promise that all groups in society would benefit from economic growth—is unobjectionable, but for countries lacking the favorable initial conditions of the HPAEs, "shared growth" may imply a much more activist government than the report allows. The report also argues that "wooing big business" (p. 181) was central to the HPAEs' success, but its conclusions on business-government relations are heavily qualified because of a fundamental ambivalence about government intervention. On the one hand, the evidence suggests that government intervention had the function of signaling or assuring the private sector of the government's benevolent intentions and building the political bases of support that were crucial for sustaining fundamental policy changes. Yet the report repeatedly emphasizes that such interventions could only work under a narrow range of conditions, and is thus hesitant to endorse them in other settings. In particular, the report stresses the importance of striking a balance between securing the confidence of the private sector and capitulating to its demands. This finding is at the heart of the discussion of "contests" and implies that, in wooing the private sector, it is crucial for the government to maintain its autonomy as well.

Other conclusions about the political foundations of the HPAEs' growth are more troubling: this underside to the miracle is addressed in the fifth part of the essay. The report is candid in admitting that repression of labor played a role in maintaining the flexibility of labor markets. However, the report downplays the broader issue of the extent to which authoritarianism was a component of the HPAE "model." It will be argued here that authoritarianism, labor repression, and growth were closely linked in a number of the Asian newly industrializing countries, and that this calls into question their relevance for newly democratizing countries. However, the relationship between repression and growth cannot be generalized and need not hold in the future or for other countries.

The essay concludes by touching briefly on the international political implications of the report. If the findings of the report are to be taken seriously, they imply a rethinking of a number of components of current World Bank strategy. Whether the rest of the developing world will be allowed to pursue an East Asian strategy—or will even be encouraged to pursue the recommendations set out in *The East Asian Miracle*—remains an open question.

. . . .

THE INHERITANCE

■   A STRONG PRESUMPTION IN THE WORLD BANK STUDY is that the HPAEs' record of sustained rapid growth with equity was the result of their economic policies. Of course, the HPAEs had not always pursued such policies: Korea and Taiwan were considered economic basket cases in the 1950s, and as recently as 1980 it was far from clear that Indonesia, Thailand, and Malaysia would join the ranks of the newly industrializing economies. Rather, changes in economic policy tended to occur simultaneously with inflections in national growth rates; there appear to be relatively clear turning points in the development histories of the HPAEs. This pattern constitutes strong prima facie evidence that policy reforms were important to the performance of the HPAEs, particularly these five larger developing ones.

This conclusion would be misleading if all five shared certain initial conditions that either directly caused the subsequent performance, facilitated subsequent reforms, or interacted with them in a positive way. As Dani Rodrik argues in his contribution to this volume, one of those initial conditions was a relatively egalitarian distribution of income. Rodrik emphasizes the positive effect that equity had on subsequent growth, but it is equally important to emphasize the effect that the *initial* distribution of income had on the *subsequent* distribution of income and on politics as well.

The World Bank study argues that rapid growth in the HPAEs was achieved with declining inequality (p. 29). There can be little doubt that rapid growth reduced the number of the poor in the HPAEs, and that growth is a necessary, if not a sufficient, condition for alleviating poverty; this point is made in the report (Table 1.1, p. 33). There are also reasons to believe that an export-oriented strategy can contribute to improvements in the *relative* distribution of income as well, particularly through its emphasis on labor-intensive, and thus labor-absorbing, products and processes. There is evidence of an improvement in equity in Korea, Taiwan, Hong Kong, and Singapore following the turn toward export-led growth, even though equity eroded somewhat in the 1980s.

However, the most important point is that much of the *present* differences in income distribution between the HPAEs and other developing countries can be explained by differences in income distribution that predate the most recent growth spurt that is the focus of the World Bank study. One explanation for these differences is in the rural social structure, and particularly the presence or absence of large landlord classes. Hong Kong and Singapore were relieved of the problem of concentrated land ownership altogether by the absence of a significant agricultural sector. The remaining HPAEs fall into two groups. Thailand and Indonesia lacked substantial indigenous landlord classes, and although there was certainly a land problem in Java, it had more to do with the extreme fragmentation of holdings than with concentrated ownership. Malaysia has the most unequal distribution of land among the HPAEs, with both foreign- and Chinese Malay-owned plantations playing an important role in the economy. However, even Malaysia has a more equal land distribution than the large Latin American countries, India, or the Philippines (see Rodrik's Table 2). Moreover, the government was dominated by a Malay leadership that was willing to act aggressively—sometimes too aggressively—to offset the inequalities arising from the initial distribution of assets.

Japan, Korea, and Taiwan, in contrast, all underwent major land reforms, each under extraordinary conditions. The land reforms in Korea and Taiwan in the immediate postwar period are reminders of the political difficulty of the task and the unusual conditions under which serious land reform emerges. Land reform was passed by the newly independent South Korean assembly under the strong political pressure of rural uprisings, the example of sweeping land reform in the northern half of the peninsula, and charges that the government was protecting the property of collaborators who had acquired or enlarged their holdings under Japanese rule. Even then, the initial distribution only covered holdings previously owned by the Japanese, and not until the peninsular war did a more complete redistribution occur.

The Taiwan case shows the critical role of political insulation in successful land reform. The Chinese Nationalists, the Kuomintang (KMT), had been completely unable to address the rural question on the mainland because of the powerful pull of the landlords. On Taiwan, however, there was no social or political connection between the KMT and indigenous elites. Having learned the lesson of the mainland, the KMT made the rural question a top priority and bulldozed opposition in the landlord-dominated provincial assembly to enact one of the most generous land reforms ever achieved in a nonrevolutionary setting.

The political as well as economic problems associated with powerful landowning classes can be seen by contrasting the Philippines with the other Southeast Asian countries, which otherwise share a number of structural similarities. Not only has the Philippine oligarchy blocked land reform, but as large landowners diversified into protected banking and manufacturing activities, they came to constitute powerful opponents to other economic and institutional reforms as well. It is not coincidental that the Philippines rivals Indonesia in the weakness of its civil service, despite the fact that it has a higher GDP per capita and a deeper educational inheritance. The decentralized nature of land-based political power and the close interpenetration between the elites and the government are important in explaining the weakness of the central government, and one that continues to plague Philippine democracy to this day.

Even to maintain a given distribution of income during a period of rapid growth cuts against expectations; that there is evidence of improvement makes the HPAEs' achievement even more remarkable. Much of what the World Bank report says about the sources of such improvement, particularly the emphasis given to education and incentives to labor-intensive production, is plausible. Yet the overall level of equality and inequality has deeper historical roots than *The East Asian Miracle* suggests. If equitable growth is a goal, the lesson of the HPAEs' experience would appear to be that concentrations of income and wealth, including wealth in land, must be attacked directly, and the sooner the better.

. . . .

HOW DID THE HPAES CHANGE DEVELOPMENT STRATEGIES? THE ROLE OF STRONG STATES

■ *THE EAST ASIAN MIRACLE* is broadly in line with other World Bank work in placing a high priority on policy reform, or what it calls "the fundamentals": stable macroeconomic policies; a realistic exchange rate; limiting price distortions in labor, capital, and goods markets, including biases against agriculture; moderating the extent of trade protection; and effective financial systems. A striking omission in the report is any discussion of how such change actually came about in the HPAEs.

The experience of the developing HPAEs shows that crises, particularly balance-of-payments crises, played an important role in leading governments to undertake such reforms. Yet their history also shows that, either before these reform episodes or contemporaneously with them, important institutional reforms occurred. Political leaders consolidated their power and centralized executive decisionmaking, but they were also willing to delegate a degree of decisionmaking power to relatively insulated technocratic agencies. In short, reform was contingent on the existence of strong states.[2]

Among the larger developing HPAEs, Taiwan and Korea were the pioneers. In Taiwan, reform came in two phases. The first was triggered by the political as well as economic disaster of the hyperinflation of the late 1940s. Forced to relocate to Taiwan following its defeat on the mainland, the KMT purged itself, centralized political power even more strongly in the hands of Chiang Kai-shek, initiated land reform, and undertook a major stabilization effort with substantial U.S. support. The new emphasis on stability was reinforced by granting the central bank substantial independence. A second phase of reform came in the late 1950s, when it became clear that the generous levels of U.S. aid would not be sustained. The government initiated a series of important exchange-rate, trade, and incentive reforms beginning in 1958. These policy changes were accompanied by additional institutional reforms that strengthened the hands of the technocrats.

The Korean story is quite similar but shows even more clearly the significance of politics. Economic policy changes did not occur until the government itself changed. The nominally democratic regime of Syngman Rhee (1948-1960) was characterized by classic rent-seeking relations with regard to trade, exchange-rate, and credit policy. Revulsion at corruption and weakening economic performance resulted in the fall of the government. Its reformist successor was too weak to push through the needed reforms and was toppled by a military coup in May 1961. The military leadership dramatically centralized political power. The economic bureaucracy was also completely restructured, and a stabilization program was initiated in 1963. Despite a formal transition to democratic rule, it was clear that President Park Chung Hee remained in charge; under his leadership the government launched a further round of trade, exchange-rate, financial, and tax reforms in 1964 and 1965.

Politics was also highly contentious in Singapore in the late 1950s, but Prime Minister Lee Kuan Yew succeeded in outmaneuvering his leftist opponents and ultimately marginalizing them completely. By 1963, Lee's People's Action Party enjoyed a virtual monopoly on political power, which it used to restructure labor organization and the bureaucracy to serve the party's political as well as developmental interests. The government's strategy was to make the city-state as attractive as possible to foreign investors. The main reform efforts centered on new incentives for multinational corporations and a controversial revamping of labor legislation to make Singapore an attractive site for offshore processing.

The World Bank report draws a sharp distinction between the Northeast and the Southeast Asian countries, particularly with respect to the conduct of industrial policy. However, the Southeast Asian HPAEs also show the significance of institutional reform for getting the "fundamentals" right, even if they did not pursue the same style of industrial policy. The pattern is most clear in Indonesia. During the late years of President Sukarno's regime, efforts by Sukarno to placate the demands of increasingly polarized political groups resulted in a reduced role for the technocrats, increased patronage, interference by the army in economic decisionmaking, and massive fiscal deficits. Stabilization came only after a military coup resulted in Suharto's assumption of power. In 1966, a group of Western-trained economists captured Suharto's ear. This group, which came to be known as the "technocrats," designed a stabilization plan that included a constitutional balanced budget provision,[3] liberalization of the capital account, and bureaucratic reorganization. The momentum of reform slowed somewhat in the mid-1970s as the oil boom promised to eliminate balance-of-payments constraints. Meanwhile a rival group of senior advisers—the "engineers," who were devoted to a more statist development strategy—gained ground, and the state-owned enterprise sector expanded dramatically. As elsewhere, the dreams built around oil wealth proved illusory. In the mid-1980s the precipitous decline in oil prices shifted power once again to the technocrats, who initiated a second round of dramatic policy reform.

Reforms in Malaysia and Thailand lack the drama of the Korean or the Indonesian case but nonetheless show the influence of crises, concentrated executive authority, and independent bureaucratic agencies. In Malaysia, macroeconomic and exchange-rate policy was generally sound in the early postindependence period, in part because of continuity in the independence of the central bank—a direct outgrowth of the currency board established under British rule. Following ethnic riots in 1969, the government moved toward a variety of interventions to favor Malays, and in the early 1980s it initiated an aggressive industrial policy. In the mid-1980s, however, the country experienced widening fiscal and balance-of-payments deficits and a dramatic slowdown in growth. In 1988, Prime Minister D. S. Mahathir bin Mohamed exploited the power of the executive to push through a set of controversial reforms that scrapped some commitments to favor Malays, began a process of privatizing state-owned enterprises, and extended attractive incentives to foreign direct investment, designed to lure new Japanese firms.

Reform in Thailand in the 1980s was more gradual, in part because the difficulties facing the economy were substantially less. Trade reform, for example, was relatively limited. Nonetheless, a rapid increase in debt in the late 1970s and the shocks of the early 1980s drove Thailand to seek World Bank assistance and forced some difficult fiscal and exchange-rate adjustments. Despite a gradual political liberalization, Prime Minister Prem Tinsulanonda maintained substantial powers vis-à-vis both the political parties and the military. For example, he could appoint unelected officials to his cabinet, and thus water down the influence of politicians. The legislature was prohibited from initiating spending bills or increasing expenditures. The bureaucracy's discretion, in turn, was circumscribed by a number of rules that limited the government's capacity to spend, and by a central bank with a long tradition of independence. The reform thrust slowed in the late 1980s under a more open and freewheeling democratic government, but a military coup in 1991 was followed by a spate of new reform decrees.

Three points emerge from these brief sketches. First, crises provided opportunities for political leaders to change course, particularly where the economic difficulties could be ascribed to previous policy. Second, reform was typically preceded by a concentration of political power in the executive, which expanded the government's freedom of maneuver. In a number of cases, including Singapore, Korea, Indonesia, and Thailand, the concentration of authority came only after a fundamental change of regime.

Perhaps the most important policy lesson for other developing countries is that executives in these HPAEs delegated at least some authority to relatively insulated technocratic agencies. Why did they choose to do this? Again, crisis conditions are an important part of the story. Typically, erratic policy and performance in previous periods had damaged the credibility of the government in the eyes of investors, bilateral donors, and the multilateral financial institutions. This loss of confidence itself constituted a significant component of the crisis. Delegation served to partly reverse this crisis of confidence by signaling the government's willingness to make certain policy decisions on the basis of economic criteria. These lessons do not imply the necessity of authoritarian rule for successful reform; adequate executive power and delegation to technocratic agencies are important components of stable and competent democratic rule as well (more on this issue below).

BUILDING SUPPORT FOR REFORM

■ EVEN IF THESE INSTITUTIONAL CHANGES did play an important role in initiating economic reform in the HPAEs, they were not enough to sustain it. A consistent finding of recent research on the political economy of reform is that reformist policies cannot be maintained unless there is an adequate base of political support.[4] This is clearly true in democracies, where party, interest group, and legislative support is critical, but it is valid for authoritarian regimes as well.

Chapter 4 of the study comes closest to providing a political analysis of how the HPAEs devised such a political formula for sustaining their high-growth policies. Some of the findings of this chapter are in need of exegesis, however, since their implications are veiled and even cut against other findings in the report. The report endorses the idea that successful policy requires political support, but it also notes that governments did not simply rely on growth to accomplish this objective. To the contrary, the study outlines a number of ways in which government intervention was crafted both to build bases of support and to actively undermine opposition. These observations suggest somewhat different and more controversial lessons about the politics of "market-friendly" policies than the report is willing to draw.

EQUITY AND POLITICAL STABILITY

Chapter 4 of *The East Asian Miracle* begins with a section titled "Achieving Legitimacy Through Shared Growth." The point of this section is that even though all the developing HPAEs had basically authoritarian governments, they managed to achieve relatively stable rule by guaranteeing that poorer social strata shared in the benefits of growth and thus provided at least tacit support for the government. The report emphasizes that this was not achieved in the fashion typical of most developing countries: "instead of granting direct income transfers or subsidizing specific commodities (for example, food or fuel), HPAE leaders have favored mechanisms that increased opportunities for upward mobility" (p. 160).

In some cases, however, these "mechanisms" involved quite extensive intervention. Land reform—a redistributive policy par excellence—was significant for the stability of authoritarian rule in Korea and Taiwan (pp. 160–61). Both governments relied on rural bases of support, particularly in Korea, where prior to the full transition to democracy in 1988 the government periodically submitted itself to controlled electoral contests. As both countries lost comparative advantage in agriculture, the governments moved aggressively to support prices and to protect the sector from low-cost imports; Japan is even more notorious in this regard. Not until the late 1980s, and then only under strong American pressure, did all three countries begin cautiously to liberalize agricultural trade, and in all three cases the political fallout was substantial.

In the city-states, where land is scarce and expensive, the provision of low-cost housing was a key to building support and even maintaining political stability. Following the social unrest of 1967, the Hong Kong government turned its attention to social welfare issues and initiated a massive housing program. In Singapore, the creation of the Housing Development Board in 1960 was one component of the People's Action Party's effort to expand its base of political support in its conflict with the left. As the report argues succinctly, "by providing low-cost housing for the majority of residents, both programs have helped to decrease inequality and minimize social unrest, thus providing the long-term stability attractive to investors" (p. 163).

In Indonesia and Malaysia, distributional policy had an ethnic dimension.[5] In both countries, Chinese minorities have wielded economic power that is highly disproportionate to their numbers. The response of political elites to this problem has been to explicitly favor "indigenous" peoples (the *bumiputra* in Malaysia, the *pribumi* in Indonesia) at the expense of the Chinese. Malaysia went the furthest in this regard. The New Economic Policy that was announced following the ethnic riots in 1969 favored Malay business and employment through quotas, demands that non-Malay businesses acquire *bumiputra* partners, the creation of state-owned enterprises that favored Malay employment, and even government-run trusts that bought up non-Malay businesses.

These three examples of building support through distributive policies—through agricultural policy, housing policy, and the favoring of ethnic groups—present a mixed record. Government intervention in housing in Hong Kong and Singapore was probably a necessity given the high price of land in the city-states. The Korean government has been forced to move in a similar direction in recent years by a political backlash against skyrocketing land prices. Land reform and government support for agriculture, particularly in Taiwan, were not just political ploys; they also contributed to growth in those two economies. Subsequent policies have increased domestic prices and had costs for consumers, but have probably not constituted a serious drag on growth. Malaysian support for the *bumiputra*, on the other hand, has created a massive state- and party-owned enterprise sector that is the source not only of inefficiency in the economy but of corruption as well. Nor is it clear that the stated objectives of reducing inequality and creating a competitive Malay private sector have been realized.

The World Bank report's emphasis on "legitimacy through shared growth" carries important implications for other countries seeking to emulate the East Asian model through policy reform. The hope of all policy reform efforts is that new groups of beneficiaries will emerge to form the nucleus of support for the program. But it is typically the case that some groups fare better than others, in the short and the long run, and that reformers need to be assured that the responses of the losers do not affect the stability of policy or of the polity itself.

The HPAEs were largely spared such concerns either because of the weak organization of the affected social groups or because authoritarian political structures allowed governments to override opposition; this issue is discussed further below. Today, however, an increasing number of developing-country governments operate under the constraints of democratic politics, usually in social settings that are much more unequal than in the HPAEs. In such settings, compensatory policy measures and attention to equity and social safety nets during the reform process are likely to be an important component of politically successful reform efforts.[6]

BUSINESS-GOVERNMENT RELATIONS

If equity is one political pillar supporting rapid growth in the HPAEs, government relations with the private sector constitute the second. It is on this critical issue that the study is most divided against itself. On the one hand, the report paints a view of the development process in which governments interact with market agents at arm's length through the manipulation of parametric instruments and incentives. This picture is little different than the Bank's traditional line: if the policy fundamentals are right, firms will respond.

On the other hand, the report presents a view of the world in which coordination problems and market failures are ubiquitous, even in functioning market economies, and in which it cannot be assumed that firms will respond vigorously to new incentives. In such a world, institutional arrangements for cooperation and information exchange are required for markets to function efficiently. Business-government relations are not at arm's length, nor is it desirable that they be. Rather, a variety of formal and informal mechanisms can facilitate communication and cooperation between the private and the public sector and improve the quality of policy.

It is this second world view that justifies the various government interventions that the report endorses, albeit cautiously. These interventions—tax incentives, preferential access to imports, and financial subsidies—are designed in part to overcome information problems. In a closed economy, not only are prices distorted, but information is lacking as well— information about design, quality, standards, packaging, and even about appropriate products. Export activities revealed ex post to be highly profitable may not be visible to companies shielded from international markets or may appear "excessively" risky. The provision of marketing information, the encouragement of foreign direct investment, and the forging of linkages with buying groups are among the ways in which the government can act to overcome this information deficit; in varying degrees all of the HPAE governments engaged in these efforts to make markets.

Yet targeted incentives provide an additional mechanism of "lowering the uncertainty associated with real investment [and] implicitly or explicitly sharing risks with the private sector" (p. 233). For example, the report finds (pp. 295–98)—and Robert Wade emphasizes in his contribution to this volume—that the HPAEs did not have particularly open trade regimes; access to *inputs*, not imports more generally, characterized early trade liberalization efforts. Korea and Taiwan, in particular, had highly bifurcated trade regimes: exporters enjoyed both the benefits of a protected position in their home market and access to low-cost inputs. The cost of both capital goods and inputs in the HPAEs was also lowered by generous financing, a central component of a successful "export-push" strategy.[7] The report's discussion of the financial systems of the HPAEs (pp. 237–241) makes it clear that much of this credit was subsidized, particularly in Korea. As Alice Amsden has argued,[8] exporters in that country faced tremendous difficulties cracking foreign markets, even after the devaluations of the early 1960s; subsidies were thus crucial to the initial export takeoff.

The World Bank study ignores the political functions of such interventions, one of which is to gain—or regain—the confidence of the private sector. A number of institutional innovations that the report hails, such as business-government deliberation councils, had the same function; they were aimed "primarily at winning the support and cooperation of business" (p. 181). First, private investors may be reluctant to respond to a given set of incentives if they think they are likely to change in the future. As the brief sketches above suggest, all of the developing HPAEs, with the possible exception of Malaysia and Hong Kong, had volatile political histories that would give both local and foreign investors pause: the predatory nature of KMT rule in the 1940s on the mainland, the chaos of the late Sukarno period in Indonesia, the political conflicts in Singapore in the late 1950s, and the inconsistency and unpredictability of Syngman Rhee's rule in Korea. Strong incentives to the private sector and the building of consultative institutions were ways for new leaders to rebuild confidence and signal government commitment to a new policy course following periods of political volatility.

There is also a second, broader political justification for the strategy of providing targeted incentives to exporters. If there are substantial economic benefits to be gained from an export-oriented model—and the report is broadly right in arguing that there are (pp. 316-324)—there are also substantial political benefits from fostering the growth and organization of the export-oriented segments of the manufacturing sector. Institutional arrangements that increase the political weight of the export sector, such as deliberation councils and exporters' associations, provide the political base for the export-oriented strategy and create mechanisms for monitoring and checking government policy. A critical factor contributing to the "flexibility" of policy in the HPAEs is precisely the sensitivity of governments to the interests of exporters and foreign investors. The Bank's reluctance to fully endorse such a portrait is not surprising; the findings suggest that the HPAEs' strategy was more mercantilist than liberal. But the report's discomfort about government intervention is not just based on economic theory; it rests ultimately on a political economy argument. A constant refrain in the report is that while government intervention may have worked in the HPAEs, it is not likely to yield the same results elsewhere because of the weakness of institutions or the likelihood that programs would get captured by rent-seeking groups (see, for example, p. 358).

This fear is partly justified and points to an important qualification on the report's enthusiasm about wooing big business. Although all of the HPAEs had conservative governments that were broadly sympathetic to private-sector interests, most also had independent and insulated bureaucracies that were partly immune from private-sector capture. More broadly, political leaderships in the HPAEs maintained a degree of political independence from the private sector.

These political conditions are central to running "contests," which the report suggests is the key mechanism used by the Northeast Asian states in particular to avoid rent seeking (pp. 93–102). The basic idea of the contest is that firms receive various supports ("rewards"), but only on the basis of clear criteria ("rules") and a mechanism of enforcement ("referees"). Clearly, a core assumption of the successful contest is that governments have enough independence and power to impose performance criteria on the favors they dispense. When they did not, the HPAEs veered toward policies that were more questionable.

Taiwan and Indonesia constitute an interesting contrast in this regard, because both are similar in having strong single-party systems. Taiwan represents the limiting case of the strong state among the HPAEs. The business community had little formal representation in the tightly organized ruling party, and technocrats were highly insulated from business interests. KMT independence was buttressed by a relatively large state-owned enterprise sector, control over finance, and the state-corporatist organization of business associations. These state-corporatist institutions generally limited the private sector's access to decision-making.

Business-government relations were not simply a result of the organizational power of the KMT party-state, however; they were also the result of the political divide that existed between the mainlander government and the local Taiwanese economic elite. In general, this divide favored the government's freedom of maneuver, since it meant that the government was relatively unconstrained by personal or family loyalties between officials and business people. Nor, given the authoritarian nature of the regime and its strong party structure, did the government depend on the business community for political support. Only with the transition to democracy have closer party-business relations emerged, to a hail of criticism that Taiwan's electoral system encourages the kind of money politics and corruption that finally toppled the Liberal Democratic Party from power in Japan.

Superficially, Indonesia appears quite similar. The Suharto regime was built on an explicitly corporatist model in which the parties—including even the ruling one—were downplayed in favor of vertical, state-sponsored interest organizations, including those for business. In contrast to Korea and Taiwan, these bodies played no discernible indus-trial policy purpose, however. The reason for this was in part the technical weakness of the bureaucracy. But it was also a function of the clientelistic linkages that developed between an important group of Chinese capitalists and the top political and military leadership. This close, symbiotic relation-ship has been the source of substantial corruption and the exchange of policy favors for political and financial support, and bears surprising simi-larity to the cronyism of the Philippines under President Ferdinand Mar-cos. That these relationships, and the corruption surrounding the presi-dent's own family, have not had more deleterious effects on the Indonesian economy can be attributed to the fact that they have not been allowed to spread, and that in other policy areas the government has been willing to delegate authority to the technocrats.

Several policy implications follow from this discussion. First, the report suggests that deliberation councils and public-private sector con-sultative mechanisms do appear to have improved the quality of policy in the countries that had them. This kind of "consultative capitalism" is one of the distinctive features of Japan's growth, in particular, although it is visible in Korea and Taiwan as well. Second, where this type of consultation has worked, it has succeeded because of the relative strength of the bureaucracies, which have had the technical competence and independence to evaluate industry claims—again, strong states mattered. Most important is the fact that bureaucracies enjoyed the *political* backing to allow them to impose conditions on any assistance extended to the private sector—a relationship Alice Amsden refers to as one of "discipline."

If these factors have influenced the performance of the HPAEs positively, they give added urgency to the report's conclusions about institution building. Rather than warn that such policies cannot work in other settings because of administrative weaknesses, it makes more sense to emphasize the importance of a strong and competent state for the formulation and implementation of coherent public policy.

. . . .

THE UNDERSIDE OF THE MIRACLE: LABOR AND AUTHORITARIANISM IN THE HPAES' GROWTH

■ THE POLITICAL UNDERSIDE OF THE MODEL HPAE comes out clearly in *The East Asian Miracle's* discussion of labor. The report corrects a common misperception, namely, that wage repression was a component of the HPAE model. Korea, Taiwan, Hong Kong, and Singapore did begin their experience with export-led growth during periods when real wage growth was stagnant. But as the economy took off, Marx's "reserve army" of under- and unemployed shrank quickly and real wages began to rise. There is no reason why Malaysia, Thailand, and even Indonesia cannot traverse a similar path. Where the government did seek to control wages directly—in Singapore—it ran up against constraints in the labor markets themselves.

The report is more frank in noting that labor repression played a role in maintaining the "flexibility" of labor markets in a number of the HPAE economies (pp. 261–273). The report does not mention the role of labor control in attracting foreign investment; this was an explicit objective of changes in the labor law that occurred in both Korea and Singapore in the late 1960s, and it appears to be an unfortunate recent development in Malaysia as well.

The report attempts to back away from these unsavory conclusions by pointing to Hong Kong and Japan as counterexamples, but the arguments are unconvincing. As the report itself notes, Hong Kong had the advantage of a continual influx of immigrants, which until recently placed downward pressure on wages and weakened union power. Japan is the one HPAE that qualifies unambiguously as a democracy, and even its postwar labor policy was forged during the conservative phase of the American occupation and contains a number of important restrictions.

The report's overview of the position of labor in the HPAEs is worth quoting at length:

> In Japan, Korea, Singapore and Taiwan, China (and to a lesser extent Malaysia), governments restructured the labor sector to suppress radical activity in an effort to ensure political stability. Governments abolished trade-based labor unions and pushed the creation of company- or enterprise-based unions. Management and company union representatives were then required to formulate and implement work-related policies. Labor movements in Indonesia and Thailand, while not subjected to systematic restructuring, were nonetheless routinely suppressed at the first sign of radicalism . . . . (pp. 164–65)

Sadly, the language of the report mimics the propaganda used by the HPAE governments themselves to justify labor repression: routine trade union activity is branded as "radicalism" that threatens "stability." Nonetheless, the report does highlight important features of the labor regimes in the HPAE countries. At the broadest political level, labor was barred from forming or aligning with political parties, or of acting collectively in the political arena at all.

With respect to systems of industrial relations, the HPAE pursued two different models. One was to fragment the union movement by prohibiting the formation of industry-wide unions and encouraging or forcing all negotiations to take place at the company level. This model in itself limited labor's clout, but it was typically accompanied by granting business management and the government a strong voice in dispute settlement. A second model, of which Korea in the 1960s and 1970s and Singapore are exemplars, was to concentrate all labor organization into one association, which was then penetrated and controlled by the government. In either case, the ability of labor to organize, strike, and bargain collectively was severely curtailed, limiting labor's ability to "interfere" in the wage-setting process.

Clearly, the lessons to be drawn with respect to labor constitute somewhat of an embarrassment. It is fair to note that unions in developing countries have often served the interests of their members at the expense of employment generation. It is also an important irony that countries whose governments have repressed labor have seen dramatic and uninterrupted increases in real wages. Yet it is neither desirable nor feasible for other developing countries to adopt the very labor regimes that the newly democratic HPAEs, Korea and Taiwan, are now dismantling. For the next generation of developing countries seeking to emulate an export-oriented strategy, new formulas for business-government-labor relations will have to be found. One hopes that these will draw on the positive lessons of the HPAE economies, such as the consistent commitment to the development of human capital. But they should also incorporate labor more closely into the political and industrial relations systems, as the small, export-oriented European countries have done, thus avoiding the abuses characteristic of labor relations in the developing HPAEs.

The treatment of labor is not the only bothersome aspect of the HPAEs' growth; there is also the broader issue of the authoritarian nature of the HPAE governments. Authoritarian rule took a number of forms and showed varying degrees of repressiveness, but was a constant across the developing HPAEs. Korea oscillated between periods of outright military rule (1961–63, 1980), highly restrictive authoritarian constitutions (1973–79, 1981–87), and limited democracy (1948–1960, 1964–1973) before experiencing a breakthrough to full democratic rule in 1987–88. Thailand has a similarly volatile political history: a long period of military rule prior to a brief democratic opening in the mid-1970s, a return to military rule, a highly controlled political liberalization during the 1980s, and another coup in 1991, followed relatively swiftly by a restoration of democratic rule.

Taiwan was a one-party system until the gradual political liberalization after 1988, although the KMT continues to dominate the island's increasingly freewheeling electoral politics. The opposition does face some restrictions, however, and the KMT still enjoys some important privileges. Indonesia remains a one-party system with an institutionalized role for the military in politics. Hong Kong is an administrative state, but with some controlled representation and a generally open atmosphere with regard to political expression.

Singapore and Malaysia are nominally democratic, but since independence, political power has been monopolized by dominant parties: the People's Action Party in Singapore and an alliance of ethnic parties in Malaysia, of which the United Malays National Organisation (UMNO) remains the *primus inter pares*. In both countries the dominant parties have used the advantages of office to thwart opposition; interestingly, it is these two dominant-party "democracies" that have swum against the regional trend toward political liberalization and democratization.

Tables 1 and 2 summarize political trends in the HPAEs, using data from Freedom House. Freedom House ranks the extent of political and civil liberties in each country; those countries that provide the most complete guarantees of these liberties are given a ranking of 1, whereas a ranking of 7 indicates the most politically closed and repressive regimes. In general, the developing HPAEs have fallen in the middle of the range; the HPAEs did not generally experience the extent of political closure and repression visible in countries receiving consistent rankings of 6 and 7. Korea and Taiwan have shown unmistakable moves toward greater openness, and Thailand appears to have returned to a more liberal path, but Malaysia, Singapore, and Indonesia show few signs of liberalization. The British colonial administration has tried desperately to institute democratic reforms in Hong Kong, but these moves have been resisted by the People's Republic of China, which already exercises a strong influence on the city-state's politics.

The debate about the relationship between authoritarianism and growth in the HPAEs remains a highly contentious one, with profound policy consequences. Bilateral aid donors and the multilateral institutions have increasingly moved toward the position that improved governance, and even democracy itself, are preconditions for growth. The Chinese leadership, in contrast, has drawn the exact opposite conclusion from the HPAE experience: economic and political reforms can be decoupled, and the economy liberalized while tight political control is maintained.

TABLE 1. POLITICAL RIGHTS IN THE HIGH PERFORMING ASIAN ECONOMIES

Year	Japan	Korea	Taiwan	Singapore	Hong Kong	Thailand	Malaysia	Indonesia
1972	2	5	6	5	n.a.	7	2	5
1974	2	5	6	5	n.a.	5	3	5
1976	2	5	5	5	n.a.	6	3	5
1978	2	5	5	5	3	6	3	5
1980	1	5	5	5	4	3	3	5
1982	1	5	5	4	4	3	3	5
1984	1	5	5	4	4	3	3	5
1986	1	4	5	4	4	3	3	5
1988	1	2	5	4	4	3	4	5
1990	1	2	3	4	4	2	5	6
1992	1	2	3	4	4	3	5	6

Notes: n.a., not available. Political rights are rights to participate meaningfully in the political process. In a democracy this means the right of all adults to vote and compete for public office, and for elected representatives to have a decisive vote on public policies. A score of 1 represents the most complete guarantees of political and civil liberties; a score of 7 indicates the most politically closed and repressive regimes. The advanced industrial democracies all have average scores of 1, 1.5, or 2.

Source: Freedom House, Freedom in the World (New York: Freedom House, various issues).

TABLE 2. CIVIL LIBERTIES IN THE HIGH PERFORMING ASIAN ECONOMIES

Year	Japan	Korea	Taiwan	Singapore	Hong Kong	Thailand	Malaysia	Indonesia
1972	1	6	5	5	n.a.	5	3	5
1974	1	6	5	5	n.a.	3	3	5
1976	1	6	5	5	n.a.	6	4	5
1978	1	5	4	5	2	4	3	5
1980	1	6	6	5	2	4	4	5
1982	1	6	5	5	2	4	4	5
1984	1	5	5	5	2	4	5	6
1986	1	5	5	5	2	3	5	6
1988	1	3	3	5	3	3	5	5
1990	1	3	3	4	3	3	4	5
1992	2	3	3	5	3	4	4	5

Notes: n.a., not available. Civil liberties are rights to free expression, to organize or demonstrate, as well as rights to a degree of autonomy such as is provided by freedom of religion, education, travel, and other personal rights. A score of 1 represents the most complete guarantees of political and civil liberties; a score of 7 indicates the most politically closed and repressive regimes. The advanced industrial democracies all have average scores of 1, 1.5, or 2.

Source: Freedom House, Freedom in the World (New York: Freedom House, various issues).

The World Bank study deals with the question in two short paragraphs (pp. 13, 187–88). In the first, it argues that, "while leaders of the HPAEs have tended to be either authoritarian or paternalistic, they have also been willing to grant a voice and genuine authority to a technocratic elite and key leaders of the private sector" (p. 13). This ignores the nature of modern authoritarianism in the developing world, which typically involves precisely an alliance between the military, portions of the private sector, and the technocrats against the left, populist forces, and labor. In the second discussion of the issue, the report asserts that the HPAEs cannot be considered authoritarian because leaders were attentive to the interests of various groups. This is again a non sequitur. Chapter 4 of the study repeatedly confuses equity with participation, suggesting that because governments paid attention to the distributional dimensions of growth, their rule was not coercive.

It is difficult to examine the history of the HPAEs dispassionately without coming to the conclusion that certain reform episodes would not have been possible without forcible changes of regime or the exercise of authoritarian power. The land reforms in Taiwan in the early 1950s, the reforms in Korea in 1961–64 and in the early 1980s, Indonesia's stabilization in the late 1960s, and many of Thailand's reforms in the 1980s constitute examples. Critical changes in the labor laws in Singapore in the mid-1960s would have faced much stiffer opposition had political conditions not changed from what they were in the late 1950s. Even in Hong Kong there are interesting episodes of the Financial Secretary resisting business requests for government support. Moreover, many of the broader institutional changes that *The East Asian Miracle* applauds, particularly the insulation of the bureaucracy, initially occurred under authoritarian auspices.

It is not clear that this history has any relevance for other developing countries. At least with respect to economic issues, the HPAEs enjoyed relatively enlightened dictatorships; it is safe to assume that such rule is generally in short supply. The problem can be seen by analyzing the strategies available to a dictator seeking to maximize personal and political power. He might achieve this objective through growth-enhancing policies, but he might also increase taxes and engage in extortion. The availability of these diametrically opposed strategies—enlightened despotism versus predatory behavior—explains why the variation in economic performance among authoritarian governments appears to be greater than among democratic ones.

A second difficulty with the authoritarian model is the assumption that authoritarian governments are independent from interest group pressures and therefore have longer time horizons. Authoritarian governments may not be accountable to electorates, but they remain vulnerable to interest group pressures and threats of instability. Indeed, the absence of regularized turnover and political competition can produce *more* pervasive and intractable corruption than would be possible under more accountable forms of rule. Indonesia and Malaysia both face this problem; in both countries the conduct of economic policy might well be improved by greater pluralism.

Nor is there reason to think that a transition to democracy will result in a deterioration of economic policy in the HPAEs, in part because past reforms have now created a broad base of support for stable, outward-oriented policies. The lesson is that democratic governments willing to undertake the combination of economic reform and industrial policy required to move domestic firms into international competition will, in the process, create new bases of political as well as economic support.

We now have important cases of democratic governments, including those of Poland, Argentina, and Bolivia, making such a leap. For other developing countries these cases hold more important and normatively appealing lessons than do the authoritarian HPAEs. Yet it is interesting that these democratic reform episodes resemble in important ways the HPAE pattern of reform described above. Crises permitted a concentration of executive authority, albeit in a democratic context, and this concentration was coupled with a certain degree of delegation to technocratic agencies.

CONCLUSION: THE INTERNATIONAL CONTEXT OF THE HPAE EXPERIENCE

■ THERE IS A FINAL INSTITUTIONAL and political dimension of the report that is saved to the very end (pp. 360–66): this is the question of the international constraints on the HPAE strategy. These constraints take two forms. The first is a fear of a fallacy of composition. The world trading system has been able to absorb the HPAEs, although at the cost of quite substantial friction; indeed, the political economy of the international trading system in the last decade can largely be written around the "Japan question" and the absorption of the developing HPAEs. Can the system absorb a whole new generation of high-performing economies pursuing export-oriented growth strategies? Not only will increased competition result in deteriorating terms of trade for the newcomers, but the political tolerance in other countries for a further flood of developing-country imports is already stretched thin.

The report is correct in downplaying these concerns. World economic growth is neither as strong nor as steady as it was during the 1950s and 1960s, when Japan and the East Asian newly industrializing countries first entered world markets. And all of the HPAEs enjoyed the advantage of access to the open and integrated American market. But the growth of world trade has remained robust, generally outpacing world GDP growth. The fear that the 1970s and 1980s would mark a return to the protectionist policies or discriminatory trading blocs of the 1930s proved unwarranted. The new protectionism has not been as significant a barrier to trade as was once expected, the General Agreement on Tariffs and Trade has survived, and those regional trading arrangements that have emerged have maintained an open character. Even if international economic and political conditions should become less propitious for trading states, this would not make the report's policy conclusions less compelling; to the contrary, the need to increase levels of investment and efficiency would become even more pressing.

The report highlights a second constraint on the HPAE model that must be taken more seriously, however: "Developing countries seeking to increase trade and attract investment will experience greater pressures to open their economies and bring their practices more closely in line with those in industrial economies" (p. 365). This pressure has taken three distinct forms. First, the upper-tier developing countries are now expected to participate more fully in the GATT system. The Tokyo Round codes pioneered the principle of conditional most-favored-nation status, and the results of the recently concluded Uruguay Round show that this idea is alive and well. Developing countries are now called on to make reciprocal concessions. Nor do regional arrangements promise a shield from such expectations—to the contrary. The North American Free Trade Agreement, the one regional agreement linking developed and developing countries, is based on reciprocal concessions rather than preferences, and indeed its negotiation involved extensive concessions from Mexico on virtually every policy issue of interest to the United States.

The second form of pressure is bilateral. The United States is the innovator in this area, but the Europeans and the Japanese are beginning to play the game as well. In the mid-1980s, American trade politics underwent an important shift, with increasing emphasis placed on efforts to open foreign markets. These efforts were not limited to the removal of traditional trade barriers but included market access for multinational firms; the entire array of new issues on the GATT agenda, from services to intellectual property to trade-related investment measures; and even issues that were not on the GATT agenda, such as the effect of industrial structure and restrictive business practices on foreign trade. The HPAEs, India, and the larger Latin American countries were the central target of these "market opening" efforts, which in fact go far beyond market opening to the question of the harmonization of national policies.

The multilateral and bilateral pressures to open markets and conform to industrial-country standards have strong implications for a number of successful strategies the HPAEs have pursued. The infant-industry protection that appears as a ubiquitous component of the larger HPAEs' trade policy would come under increasing pressure. Dumping, narrowly conceived, as well as the broader practice of cross-subsidizing exports through protection of the domestic market for the same goods, would be more tightly controlled. Subsidies of all sorts would be subjected to tighter bilateral, if not international, scrutiny. Export and local content requirements on foreign firms would be eliminated as an industrial policy tool. The report's discussion of the HPAEs' "openness to technology" fails to underline the importance of reverse engineering and outright pirating in their success. Under new intellectual property laws, copyrights, patents, trademarks, and computer software will enjoy toughened protection, foreclosing this strategy for the next generation of developing economies. Even the ability to use the financial system for the purposes outlined in the report might be limited by pressures to open the services sector to foreign competition and to liberalize the capital account. In short, a central question is whether international politics will allow a replication of the HPAE strategy as outlined in the study.

In answering this question, we come finally to the third source of policy pressure on the developing countries: the multilateral institutions themselves. The severe balance-of-payments and debt crises experienced by many developing countries during the 1980s naturally strengthened the hands of foreign creditors, including the multilateral ones. The World Bank and the International Monetary Fund did not succeed in getting developing countries to live up to all the terms of conditional lending set out in stand-by, structural, and sectoral adjustment loans. Nonetheless, the influence of these institutions was substantial.

The publication of the report thus presents us with an opportunity for a natural experiment. Did the entire exercise only serve to confirm what the Bank already believed, in which case we can expect no change in the terms and conditions of Bank lending? Or will the new lessons derived from the East Asian cases—on the importance of equity, on the importance of strengthening state institutions—now be reflected in revamped World Bank programs? The answer to this question will constitute the true test of the significance—and sincerity—of the *The East Asian Miracle*.

Notes

The author thanks Ed Campos, Albert Fishlow, Peter Gourevitch, Catherine Gwin, and Dani Rodrik for comments on earlier drafts.

[1] A portion of the report's Chapter 2 (pp. 93–102) on public policy is devoted to the question of how government intervention can be designed to avoid rent seeking and capture by special interests, and the entirety of Chapter 4 is on the institutional basis of growth.

[2] Hong Kong is no exception to this rule. Its economic policies were guided by a highly insulated colonial bureaucracy—a solution that is of little relevance to other countries. On the role of the state in the East Asian newly industrializing countries, see Stephan Haggard, *Pathways from the Periphery: The Politics of Growth in the Newly Industrializing Countries* (Ithaca, NY: Cornell University Press, 1990).

[3] The concept of "balance" was a bit unusual, however: expenditures could not exceed the sum of revenues plus counterpart funds generated by the aid program.

[4] See Stephan Haggard and Robert Kaufman, "Introduction: Institutions and Economic Policy," in *The Politics of Adjustment*, Stephan Haggard and Robert Kaufman, eds. (Princeton, NJ: Princeton University Press, 1992).

[5] In Thailand, the government accommodated the ethnic Chinese community, and it became closely integrated into Thai society.

[6] Carol Graham, "Market Transitions and the Poor: Comparative Studies in Sustaining Reform," unpublished manuscript, Brookings Institution, Washington, DC, June 1993.

[7] Colin I. Bradford, Jr., *From Trade-Driven Growth to Growth-Driven Trade: Reappraising the East Asian Development Experience* (Paris: OECD Development Centre, 1994).

[8] Alice H. Amsden, *Asia's Next Giant* (New York: Oxford University Press, 1989).

About the Authors

ALBERT FISHLOW, professor of economics and dean of International and Area Studies at the University of California, Berkeley, is chairman of ODC's Program Advisory Group. Currently he also serves as the coeditor of the *Journal of Development Economics* and as member of Issues in Democratization of the National Research Council; the Advisory Board of the Center for European Studies of the Hungarian Academy of Sciences; and the Social Science Research Council Committee on Problems and Policy; and the Committee on Peace and Security, among others. From 1975-76, he served as Deputy Assistant Secretary of State for Inter-American Affairs. In addition to serving as a consultant to the World Bank, United Nations, and several foundations including The Rockefeller Foundation and The Ford Foundation, he has also written many articles and books. Among his most recent publications are "The Macroeconomics of the Brazilian External Debt," in *Developing Country Debt and Economic Performance* (University of Chicago Press, 1990); and "Latin American Economic Development: 1950–80" (with Eliana Cardoso) in *Journal of Latin American Studies.*

CATHERINE GWIN is vice president for studies at the Overseas Development Council and directs ODC's Policy Studies Program. Most recently she served as special program advisor to the Rockefeller Foundation. She has consulted for The Rockefeller Foundation and The Ford Foundation, the Asia Society, Columbia University, and the United Nations, among others. Previously, she was senior associate at the Carnegie Endowment, North/South issues coordinator for the U.S. International Development Cooperation Agency, and executive director of the 1980s Project of the Council of Foreign Relations. Her publications include *Pulling Together: The International Monetary Fund in a Multipolar World* (ODC, 1989); and "International Development Assistance: The Agencies, Policies, and Issues" (The Curry Foundation, 1988).

STEPHAN HAGGARD is a professor at the Graduate School of International Relations and Pacific Studies, University of California, San Diego, as well as a member of ODC's Program Advisory Committee. He has written many articles and books including *Pathways from the Periphery: The Political Economy of Growth in the Newly Industrializing Countries* (Cornell University Press, 1990); *The Politics of Adjustment* (Princeton University Press, 1992); *The Political Econ-*

omy of Finance in Developing Countries (Cornell University Press, 1993); and *Voting for Reform: The Politics of Adjustment in New Democracies* (Oxford University Press, 1994). He is currently completing a manuscript with Robert Kaufman entitled *The Political Economy of Democratic Transitions.* He has been a consultant to USAID, the World Bank, and the Organisation for Economic Co-operation and Development.

DANI RODRIK is professor of economics and international affairs at Columbia University and a program associate of the Overseas Development Council. He is also a research associate of the National Bureau of Economic Research, a research fellow of the Centre for Economic Policy Research, and senior research fellow of the Institute for Policy Reform. He is the co-author of *Eastern Europe and the Soviet Union in the World Economy* (1991), co-editor of *The Economics of Middle East Peace* (1993), and author of many articles on trade policy, economic development, and political economy in professional journals.

ROBERT WADE is a fellow of the Institute of Development Studies at Sussex University and a member of ODC's Program Advisory Group. He has been a visiting professor at Princeton University, Massachusetts Institute of Technology, and the University of California, San Diego. He has also been a consultant to the U.S. Congress and the World Bank and a fellow at Duke University and the Woodrow Wilson Center for Scholars. His many publications include *Governing the Market: Economic Theory and the Role of Government in East Asian Industrialization* (Princeton University Press, 1990); *Village Republics: Economic Conditions for Collective Action in South India* (Cambridge University Press, 1988); and *Inside Strong and Weak States: State Capacity, Economic Growth, and Muddy Water—India and Korea* (forthcoming 1994).

About the ODC

ODC fosters an understanding of how development relates to a much changed U.S. domestic and international policy agenda and helps shape the new course of global development cooperation.

ODC's programs focus on three main issues: the challenge of political and economic transitions and the reform of development assistance programs; the development dimensions of international responses to global problems; and the implications of development for U.S. economic security.

In pursuing these themes, ODC functions as:

■ *A center for policy analysis.* Bridging the worlds of ideas and actions, ODC translates the best academic research and analysis on selected issues of policy importance into information and recommendations for policymakers in the public and private sectors.

■ *A forum for the exchange of ideas.* ODC's conferences, seminars, workshops, and briefings bring together legislators, business executives, scholars, and representatives of international financial institutions and nongovernmental groups.

■ *A resource for public education.* Through its publications, meetings, testimony, lectures, and formal and informal networking, ODC makes timely, objective, nonpartisan information available to an audience that includes but reaches far beyond the Washington policymaking community.

ODC is a private, nonprofit organization funded by foundations, corporations, governments, and private individuals.

Stephen J. Friedman is the Chairman of the Overseas Development Council, and John W. Sewell is the Council's President.

Board of Directors

Program Advisory Group

Overseas Development Council

SPECIAL PUBLICATIONS SUBSCRIPTION OFFERS

U.S.-Third World Policy Perspectives • Policy Essays • Policy Focus

Subscribe to ODC's 1994 publications series and you will receive an invaluable source of independent analyses of U.S.-Third World issues—economic, political, and social—at a savings of over 15% off the regular price.

ODC's **U.S.-Third World Policy Perspectives** series brings 6–9 different perspectives presenting creative new policy options or insights into the implications of existing policy. Perspectives for 1994 include *Population and Development: Old Debates, New Conclusions* by Robert Cassen and contributors, and *Intricate Links: Democratization and Market Reforms in Latin America and Eastern Europe,* by Joan M. Nelson with contributing chapters from experts from both regions.

Policy Essays explore critical issues on the U.S.-Third World agenda in 80–120 succinct pages, offering concrete recommendations for action. This subscription will bring you the first six essays in 1994.

Essay topics will include the current population and development debate, democratization and ethnic nationalism in Africa and Eastern Europe, sustainable agriculture, and a comparison of savings and exchange rates in East Asia and Latin America.

Brief and easy to read, each **Policy Focus** briefing paper provides background information and analysis on a current topic on the policy agenda. In 1994, 6–8 papers will cover issues such as the environment and international trade, poverty and gender, the global threat of AIDS, and U.S. policy toward the multilateral development banks, among others.

1994 SUBSCRIPTION OPTIONS*

U.S.-Third World Policy Perspectives	$35.00
Policy Essay	$65.00
Policy Focus	$20.00

* Subscribers will receive publications issued to date upon receipt of payment; other publications will be sent upon release. Book-rate postage is included.

All orders require prepayment. Visa and Mastercard orders accepted by phone or mail. Please send check or money order to:

O | D | C

Publication Orders
Overseas Development Council
1875 Connecticut Avenue, NW
Suite 1012-PE
Washington, DC 20009